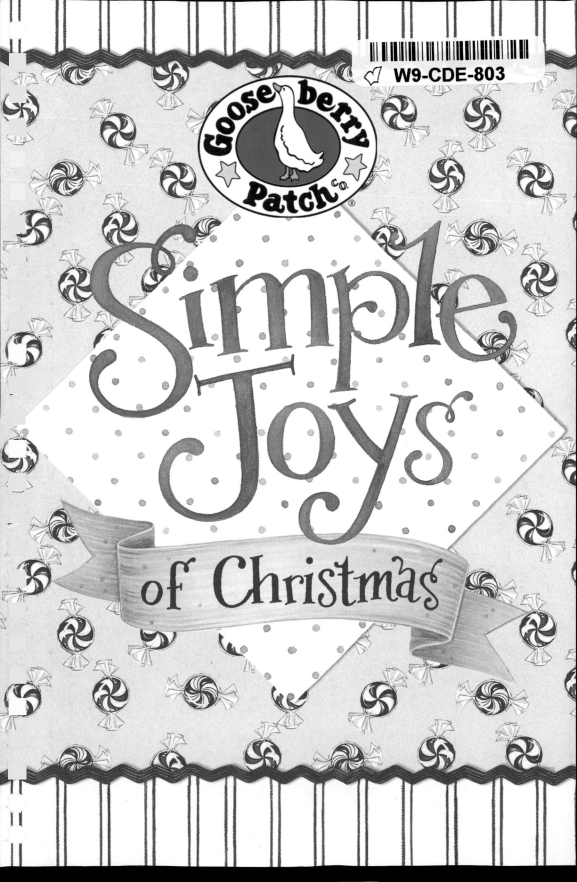

Gooseberry Patch Co.

# Simple Joys

## of Christmas

A Country Store In Your Mailbox®

Gooseberry Patch
600 London Road
Department BOOK
Delaware, OH 43015

★

1-800-854-6673
gooseberrypatch.com

Copyright 2001, Gooseberry Patch 1-888052-88-0
First Printing, October, 2001

## How To Subscribe

Would you like to receive
"A Country Store in Your Mailbox"®?
For a 2-year subscription to our 96-page
**Gooseberry Patch** catalog, simply send $3.00 to:

Gooseberry Patch
600 London Road
Department BOOK
Delaware, OH 43015

# Contents

Take time to LAUGH,
it's the music of the soul.

—Unknown

# Dedication

For those who know that the love of
family & friends is the best possible
Christmas present.

# Appreciation

For all the sweet memories shared with
us...thank you for making this book
one from the heart.

# Blessings

*Sharing memories from the heart...*

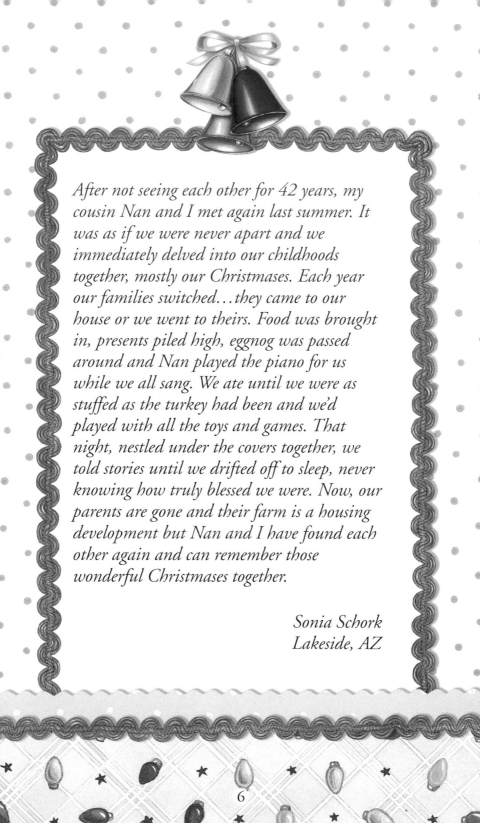

*After not seeing each other for 42 years, my cousin Nan and I met again last summer. It was as if we were never apart and we immediately delved into our childhoods together, mostly our Christmases. Each year our families switched…they came to our house or we went to theirs. Food was brought in, presents piled high, eggnog was passed around and Nan played the piano for us while we all sang. We ate until we were as stuffed as the turkey had been and we'd played with all the toys and games. That night, nestled under the covers together, we told stories until we drifted off to sleep, never knowing how truly blessed we were. Now, our parents are gone and their farm is a housing development but Nan and I have found each other again and can remember those wonderful Christmases together.*

*Sonia Schork*
*Lakeside, AZ*

# Festive Cheese Ball

2 8-oz. pkgs. cream
  cheese, softened

2 c. grated Cheddar
  cheese

1 T. onion, finely
  chopped

1 T. pimento, finely
  chopped

1 T. green pepper,
  finely chopped

2 t. Worcestershire
  sauce

1 t. lemon juice

1/8 t. salt

1/8 t. cayenne pepper

1/2 c. chopped walnuts

In a medium bowl, blend cheeses together with a
fork. Mix in remaining ingredients except the
walnuts. Place mixture in plastic wrap and shape
into a ball; chill thoroughly or overnight. Roll in
chopped walnuts and serve with crackers. Makes
4 cups.

*I have always loved Christmas and, for the last few years, Mommaw had given each of the girls in our family a doll for Christmas. Every year, I'd just put it aside and finally, I asked instead for something of hers that she felt like parting with. The dolls stopped coming and I received a tablecloth that was her mothers, a doily she had made and a piece of jewelry. She would pin a little note on these precious gifts telling me where they came from and how old they were. Each one, with its little note, has been safely packed away in my cedar chest for my daughter. Each time I see them, I remember the special times I spent with her. After she passed away last June, I realized that the dolls we received each year were her way of trying to keep her granddaughters small. There's not a day that goes by that I don't think of her. Each Christmas, I plan to take one item out of my cedar chest to remind me of that very special person who quietly slipped out of my life. Everyone should have a grandmother as wonderful as mine was.*

*Tina Goodpasture*
*Meadowview, VA*

# Blessings

## Fruit Chill

**3-oz. pkg. fruit-
    flavored gelatin**
**1 c. boiling water**
**1 pt. vanilla ice cream,
    softened**

**15-oz. can fruit
    cocktail, drained**

Dissolve gelatin in boiling water; set aside. Stir ice cream and fruit cocktail together; mix into gelatin mixture. Pour into a 4-cup mold; refrigerate until firm. Makes 6 to 8 servings.

With Love

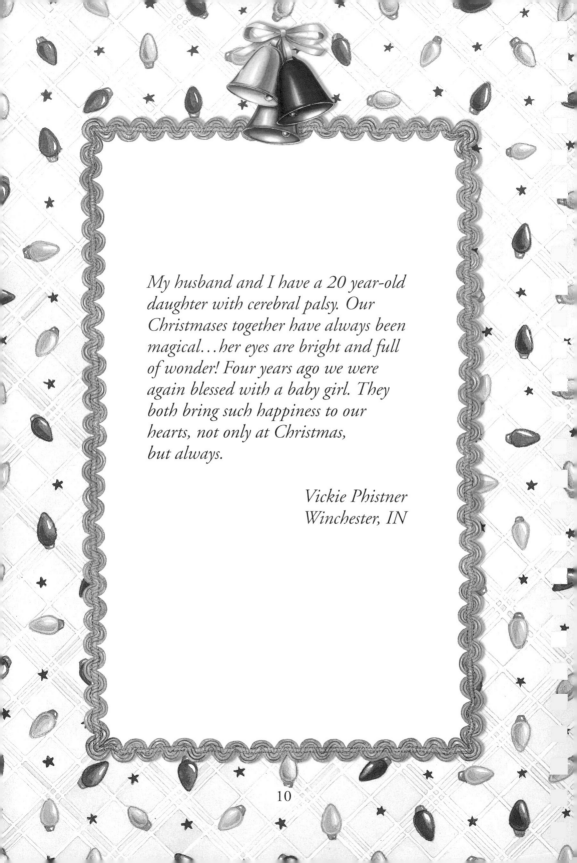

*My husband and I have a 20 year-old daughter with cerebral palsy. Our Christmases together have always been magical…her eyes are bright and full of wonder! Four years ago we were again blessed with a baby girl. They both bring such happiness to our hearts, not only at Christmas, but always.*

*Vickie Phistner*
*Winchester, IN*

# Blessings

## Magical Christmas Cookies

Combine sugar, brown sugar and margarine or butter; beat until fluffy. Add vanilla and eggs; blend well. Add flour, baking soda and salt; mix well. Stir in oats, chocolate bits and raisins. Drop dough by 1/4 cupfuls, 3 inches apart, on an ungreased baking sheet. Bake at 325 degrees for 18 to 22 minutes or until golden. Cool 2 minutes on baking sheet. Makes about 2 dozen cookies.

### Ingredients:

3/4 c. sugar

3/4 c. brown sugar, packed

1 c. margarine or butter

2 t. vanilla extract

2 eggs, beaten

1-2/3 c. all-purpose flour

1 t. baking soda

1/2 t. salt

2 c. quick-cooking oats, uncooked

2 c. colorful, candy-coated chocolate mini baking bits

1 c. raisins

11

The Christmas of 1992 will always be a very special Christmas to me. That year, my mother was diagnosed with Parkinson's disease. After she was released from the hospital, unable to care for herself and return home, she entered a nursing facility. I had come to terms with the fact that this was probably where she would spend the rest of her life. Thankfully, she responded well to the medication and, after much hard work and determination on her part, she was able to return home. That same year, one of our 2 miniature Schnauzers developed a health problem. Because my husband and I don't have any children, these two wonderful animals are a very special part of our family. We were devastated to think that we might lose one of them. However, thanks to a terrific veterinarian we got through the problem successfully. With the bad times behind us and heading into the holiday season, I decided to make that Christmas the best one ever. Each Christmas since then, my mind is flooded with memories of how truly blessed we were to have been given not one, but two happy endings.

Susan Helms
Beaver Falls, PA

# Blessings

## Fairy Drops

4-1/2 c. all-purpose flour
1 t. baking soda
1 t. cream of tartar
1 t. salt
1 c. butter
1 c. powdered sugar
1 c. sugar
1 c. oil
2 eggs
2 t. almond extract
Garnish: crushed candy canes

Stir together flour, baking soda, cream of tartar and salt; set aside. Using an electric mixer, beat butter on medium-low speed until smooth. Add powdered sugar and sugar; beat until fluffy. Beat in oil, eggs and almond extract until just combined. With mixer on medium speed, gradually add dry ingredients, then cover and chill dough 30 minutes. Roll teaspoonfuls of dough into balls. Arrange balls on an ungreased baking sheet and gently flatten to about 1/4-inch thickness using the bottom of a glass. Bake at 350 degrees for 10 to 12 minutes or until edges are light brown. Remove from cookie sheet and let cool completely on a wire rack; frost and top with crushed candy canes if desired. Makes about 5 dozen cookies.

## Frosting:

1/2 c. butter
1/2 t. almond extract
1/2 t. vanilla extract
2-1/2 to 3-1/2 c. powdered sugar
3 T. light cream or milk

Beat butter until fluffy; add extracts. Blend in powdered sugar alternately with cream or milk; beat until smooth. Makes 2 cups.

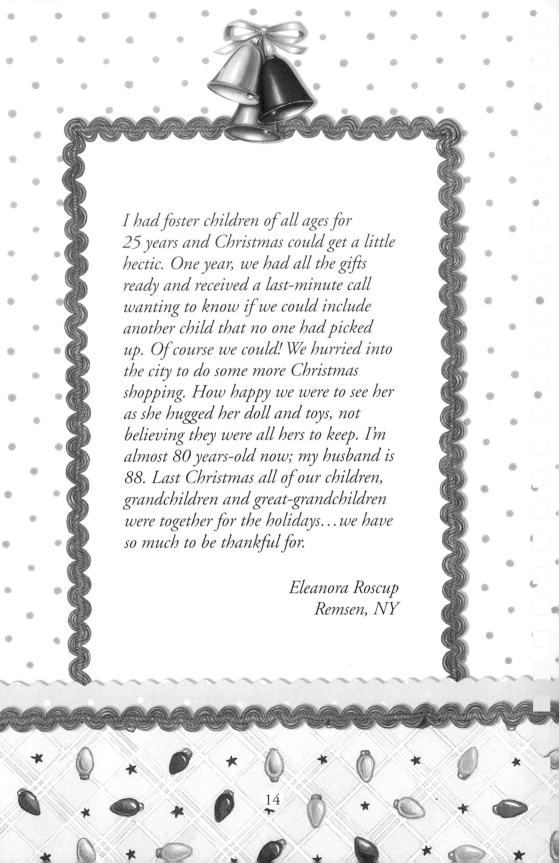

*I had foster children of all ages for 25 years and Christmas could get a little hectic. One year, we had all the gifts ready and received a last-minute call wanting to know if we could include another child that no one had picked up. Of course we could! We hurried into the city to do some more Christmas shopping. How happy we were to see her as she hugged her doll and toys, not believing they were all hers to keep. I'm almost 80 years-old now; my husband is 88. Last Christmas all of our children, grandchildren and great-grandchildren were together for the holidays…we have so much to be thankful for.*

*Eleanora Roscup*
*Remsen, NY*

## Chocolate No-Bake Cookies

1/2 c. margarine
1/2 c. milk
4 T. baking cocoa
2 c. sugar
1 t. vanilla extract

1/2 c. smooth peanut butter
3 c. quick-cooking oats, uncooked

Mix margarine, milk and cocoa together in a saucepan. Bring to a boil and continue to boil for 1-1/2 minutes. Add sugar, vanilla, peanut butter and oats; stir well. Drop by teaspoonfuls onto wax paper. Let cool to harden. Makes about 2 dozen cookies.

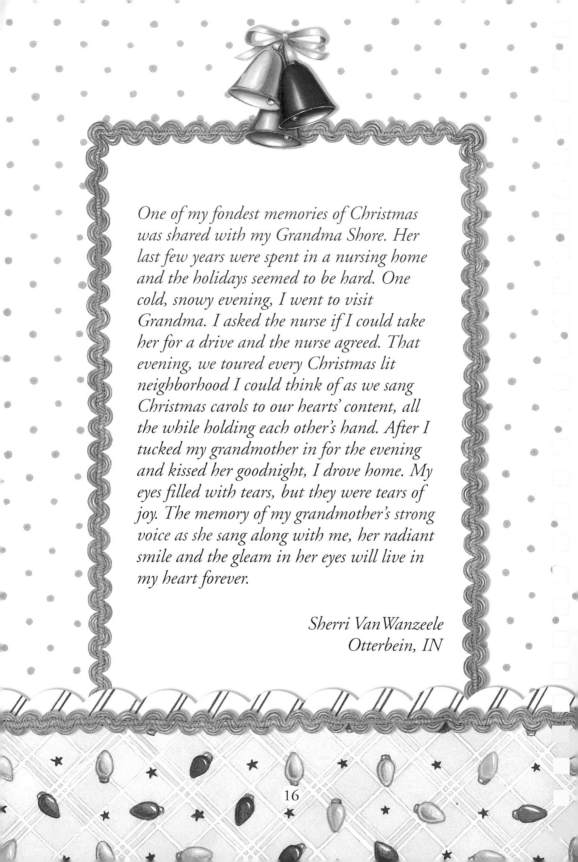

One of my fondest memories of Christmas was shared with my Grandma Shore. Her last few years were spent in a nursing home and the holidays seemed to be hard. One cold, snowy evening, I went to visit Grandma. I asked the nurse if I could take her for a drive and the nurse agreed. That evening, we toured every Christmas lit neighborhood I could think of as we sang Christmas carols to our hearts' content, all the while holding each other's hand. After I tucked my grandmother in for the evening and kissed her goodnight, I drove home. My eyes filled with tears, but they were tears of joy. The memory of my grandmother's strong voice as she sang along with me, her radiant smile and the gleam in her eyes will live in my heart forever.

Sherri VanWanzeele
Otterbein, IN

# Pineapple Ham Loaf

2 eggs, beaten
1/2 c. milk
1 c. round, buttery
   crackers, crushed
1/4 t. pepper
1 lb. ground pork
1-1/2 lbs. cooked ham,
   ground
1 c. brown sugar,
   packed

1 t. dry mustard
1/3 c. apple cider
   vinegar
1/4 c. water
8-oz. can crushed
   pineapple,
   undrained

Blend together eggs, milk, crackers and pepper; add
pork and ham, mixing well. Form into a loaf and
place in a 9"x5" loaf pan. Combine brown sugar,
mustard, vinegar, water and pineapple, blending
well; pour over ham loaf. Bake, uncovered, at
350 degrees for 1-1/2 hours or until a meat
thermometer registers 170 degrees. Baste frequently
during baking time. Makes 6 to 8 servings.

Simple joys...the special days before Christmas when each heart is filled with love and the desire to give to others. The sparkling diamonds of snow that appear as you race down the hill on your sled. The twinkling lights you notice as you walk down the streets with the one you love. The cozy feeling sitting around the fireplace munching on goodies baked for your family. The Christmas service surrounded by loved ones and friends. These are the true and simple joys of Christmas.

Frances Stutzman
Dalton, OH

# Blessings

## Fireside Dip

Blend ingredients together in the top of a double boiler. Stir gently over medium heat until mixture is thoroughly combined. Serve warm with tortilla chips. Makes 10 to 12 servings.

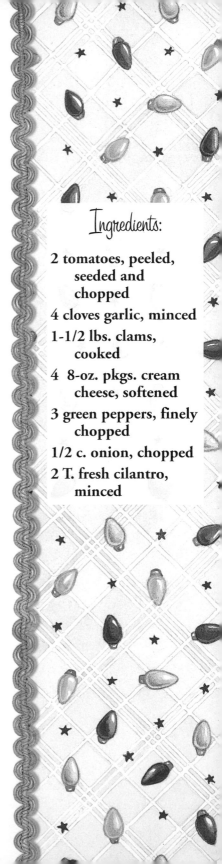

### Ingredients:

2 tomatoes, peeled, seeded and chopped

4 cloves garlic, minced

1-1/2 lbs. clams, cooked

4  8-oz. pkgs. cream cheese, softened

3 green peppers, finely chopped

1/2 c. onion, chopped

2 T. fresh cilantro, minced

*I'm the oldest of 6 children and, at times, it wasn't easy for my parents to get us the extra things we wanted after the necessities were taken care of. I was in junior high school and not really feeling like I "fit in" that particular year. The holiday season was coming and I really wanted a white, fluffy sweater like all the other girls were wearing. I remember telling my father that the sweater was the only thing I wanted. On Christmas morning, it was hectic as usual. Wrapping paper was everywhere as my little brothers and younger sister unwrapped things they needed as well as the toys that my father always made sure we all got. I remember looking for a box that would hold the one thing I wanted so desperately. I found it and unwrapped it while my father looked on with a smile. When I opened the box and saw the sweater, I was a little surprised and looked up at my dad. The look on his face stopped whatever I was thinking from coming out of my mouth. He was so pleased with what he had picked out just for me and I could see the love in his eyes. A white sweater with pink, yellow and blue flowers on the front was the best gift I could get from my father because he picked it out with so much love. I learned a lot that Christmas and now I try to choose Christmas gifts with the love that my father taught me so many years ago.*

*Jayne McGeary*
*Altoona, PA*

# Blessings

## Walnut-Pumpkin Cookies

| | |
|---|---|
| 1 c. shortening or butter | 1 t. baking powder |
| 1 c. sugar | 1 t. baking soda |
| 1 egg, beaten | 1 t. cinnamon |
| 1 c. canned pumpkin | 1/2 t. salt |
| 1 t. vanilla extract | 1/2 c. raisins |
| 2 c. all-purpose flour | 1/2 c. chopped walnuts |

Cream together shortening or butter and sugar. Blend in egg, pumpkin and vanilla; set aside. Sift together flour, baking powder, baking soda, cinnamon and salt; add to creamed mixture. Fold in raisins and nuts; drop by teaspoonfuls on a greased baking sheet. Bake at 375 degrees for 8 to 10 minutes; ice when cool. Makes 4 dozen.

## Icing:

| | |
|---|---|
| 3 T. butter | 1 c. powdered sugar |
| 4 T. milk | 3/4 t. vanilla extract |
| 1/2 c. brown sugar, packed | |

Combine first 3 ingredients in a saucepan. Bring to a boil and cook 2 minutes; let cool. Stir in powdered sugar and vanilla, blending well.

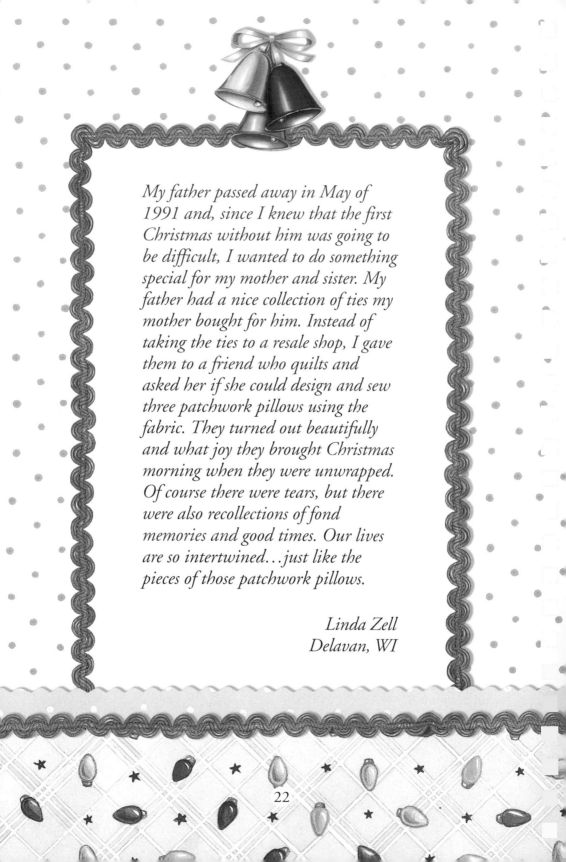

*My father passed away in May of 1991 and, since I knew that the first Christmas without him was going to be difficult, I wanted to do something special for my mother and sister. My father had a nice collection of ties my mother bought for him. Instead of taking the ties to a resale shop, I gave them to a friend who quilts and asked her if she could design and sew three patchwork pillows using the fabric. They turned out beautifully and what joy they brought Christmas morning when they were unwrapped. Of course there were tears, but there were also recollections of fond memories and good times. Our lives are so intertwined…just like the pieces of those patchwork pillows.*

*Linda Zell*
*Delavan, WI*

22

## Anniversary Punch

46-oz. can apple juice

12-oz. can frozen
orange juice
concentrate,
thawed

46-oz. can pineapple
juice

2 qts. ginger ale

Combine apple juice, orange juice and pineapple juice until well blended. Add ginger ale and stir to mix. Makes 40 servings.

*It was December in South Africa and my husband and I were missionaries. What was our holiday season was the midst of summer in Africa and many people were heading for the beach. That year, it seemed that we had not only left family & friends behind, but also our Christmas traditions which were a special part of our lives. My first inclination was to just concentrate on the spiritual side of Christmas. I reasoned that we shouldn't spend our living allowance on such frivolous things as decorations and gifts. I think I could have kept my resolve if it weren't for what I found tucked in the back of a dark closet. We uncovered a scrawny little artificial tree, one string of lights and a box of used but neatly folded, wrapping paper. These were the legacy of unknown missionary couples who had gone before us. In the following week, every spare moment was spent creating something. My years spent as a kindergarten teacher began to show and ornaments were born of paper and found objects from around the apartment. Goodies from our kitchen were made for new friends and we felt the spirit of Christmas emerging from within. At the end of the season, I reluctantly took down the homemade decorations and packed them tenderly away with the scrawny little tree, strand of lights and gently used wrapping paper. As for the decorations, they would remain for some future missionary couple to discover in the back of a closet on a hot December day.*

*Ruth Palmer*
*Glendale, UT*

24

# Blessings

## Best-Ever Popcorn Balls

14-oz. can sweetened
    condensed milk
1/2 c. margarine

1 lb. brown sugar
1 c. corn syrup
12 qts. popped popcorn

Combine milk, margarine, brown sugar and corn
syrup in a saucepan over low heat. Stir constantly to
keep mixture from scorching. When mixture reaches
234 to 240 degrees on a candy thermometer, or the
soft ball stage, remove saucepan from heat. Pour
mixture over popcorn; stir well to make sure popcorn
is coated. Butter hands well, then shape mixture into
balls. Makes over 2 dozen large popcorn balls.

*The first time I went to a department store as a child and saw a Christmas tree, I wanted a tree as beautiful as the one I'd seen. Everything was perfect…matching bows and huge glass ball ornaments all perfectly arranged on the tree. Now, as a wife and mother, I have the perfect tree each year. It's decorated with cowboys, dolls and ornaments made in school…ones given to my children with their names on them and even fishing bobbers adorn my tree. Each year, as my children decorate the tree with their beloved ornaments, I often think that we do have the most beautiful tree…a tree decorated with love, family and ornaments made from the heart.*

*Angela Venable*
*Gooseberry Patch*

# Blessings

## Harvest Fruit & Nut Pie

Blend together apples, cranberries, pineapple, walnuts and sugar; stir well. Sift together brown sugar, flour, cinnamon and nutmeg; add to apple mixture. Divide equally between 2 pie crusts; dot each with butter and cover with top pie crust. Bake at 400 degrees for 45 minutes. Makes 2 pies.

### Ingredients:

4 Granny Smith apples, peeled and sliced

1 c. cranberries

1/2 c. pineapple tidbits

1/2 c. chopped walnuts

1 c. sugar

2/3 c. brown sugar, packed

4 T. all-purpose flour

1 t. cinnamon

1/4 t. nutmeg

4  9-inch deep dish pie crusts

3 T. butter

When I was a little girl in the 1940's, we didn't receive fancy gifts like kids receive now. We had puzzles, spinning tops, a diary with its own key, coloring books, crayons, a harmonica or a doll. We were so thrilled and excited over what Santa was going to bring us, we could hardly sleep the night before. It's not the price of the gift that counts, it's the love with which it's given. Christmas is about the golden moments we share with those we love. My daughter-in-law says she has never seen anyone love Christmas as much as I do. Christmas is a promise kept. Christmas is hope. Christmas can be magical when we surround ourselves with a very special kind of love…a love based on doing simple things together. This is what makes our lives sweet and fills us with countless wonder.

Judy Borecky
Escondido, CA

# Yummy Waffles

1/2 c. butter
2 c. biscuit baking mix
1 egg

1-1/4 c. club soda
1/2 T. lemon zest

Whisk all ingredients together until well blended. Coat a waffle iron with non-stick vegetable spray and spoon in batter. Continue cooking until steam ceases. Repeat with remaining batter. Makes about 4 servings.

*When my husband and I were first married and just starting out, money for Christmas presents was tight. Looking out my window one cool, crisp morning, I got an idea. We had an old apple tree filled with beautiful apples in the yard. My father had always loved apple butter when I was a child but it wasn't easy to find. Never having canned before, I made my first batch, covered the jar lids with fabric and tied them with strands of raffia. My simple gift was so well received, I've been asked to repeat it for the last 19 years! Gifts don't have to come from a store when they come from the heart.*

*Dayna Hansen*
*Junction City, OR*

# Blessings

## Dad's Spiced Apple Butter

8 to 10 Rome, Braeburn or Granny Smith apples, peeled and quartered
1/2 c. apple juice or water
2 T. lemon juice

3/4 c. sugar
1 t. cinnamon
1/8 t. ground cloves
1/8 t. salt
1/8 t. allspice
1/8 t. nutmeg

Place apples in a slow cooker; add juice or water and lemon juice. Sprinkle on all remaining ingredients; stir. Cover and cook on low 8 hours or on high 3 to 4 hours. Stir and mash apples occasionally throughout cooking time. Ladle apple butter into 6 hot, sterilized half-pint jars. Add sterilized lid and tighten down ring. Fill a large pan with enough water to completely cover the jars; bring water to a boil. Place jars in the boiling water bath for 10 minutes. Remove jars and allow to cool. Jar lids will "ping" as each seals and will appear slightly indented. Makes 6 half-pint jars.

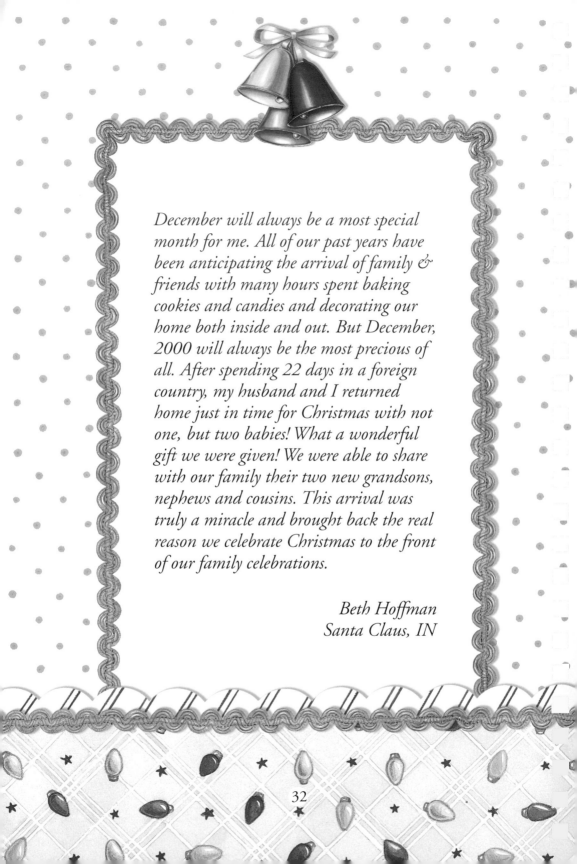

*December will always be a most special month for me. All of our past years have been anticipating the arrival of family & friends with many hours spent baking cookies and candies and decorating our home both inside and out. But December, 2000 will always be the most precious of all. After spending 22 days in a foreign country, my husband and I returned home just in time for Christmas with not one, but two babies! What a wonderful gift we were given! We were able to share with our family their two new grandsons, nephews and cousins. This arrival was truly a miracle and brought back the real reason we celebrate Christmas to the front of our family celebrations.*

*Beth Hoffman*
*Santa Claus, IN*

# Sugar-Topped Coffee Cake

1 pkg. active dry yeast
1/4 c. warm water
1/2 c. plus 1 T. sugar,
   divided
3/4 c. butter, divided

1 c. milk, scalded
2 eggs, beaten
1 t. salt
5 c. all-purpose flour
1/4 t. cinnamon

Dissolve yeast in water; set aside. Add 1/2 cup sugar and 1/2 cup butter to milk; let cool to lukewarm then add to yeast mixture. Blend eggs and salt with yeast mixture; stir in 3 cups flour with an electric mixer. Blend 10 minutes, then stir in remaining flour by hand. Dough will be soft and sticky. Divide mixture between two lightly greased 9" round cake pans; let rise 30 to 45 minutes. Mix remaining butter, sugar and cinnamon together; sprinkle over batter. Bake at 400 degrees for 20 minutes. Makes 16 servings.

*When our youngest son, Russ, was 9 years-old, he really didn't seem to have the Christmas spirit that he'd had in years past. I gave him a pen and some paper and asked that he draw me a picture of what he thought of when I said "Christmas." He drew a decorated Christmas tree. I took that drawing to a printer and had it made into a greeting card, complete with a holiday wish inside. I even gave Russ credit for the card design on the back…he was delighted! It became a tradition for him to draw our cards for many years after that. Sadly, we lost Russ when he was 19 years-old. I have had the cards reproduced and still use them. His name appears on the cards along with a special little note that says "For several years, prior to his death, Russ drew our Christmas cards. To honor his memory, these cards have been reprinted, exactly as the originals." This has become one of the most precious joys of Christmas for my entire family.*

*Charlotte Wolf*
*Ft. Lauderdale, FL*

# Blessings

## Sweet Nothings

Melt butter, peanut butter and chocolate chips over medium heat. Pour cereal in a large bowl; top with chocolate mixture. Stir gently until well coated. Slowly pour powdered sugar over snack mix and stir until blended. Spread evenly on a baking sheet to cool; store in an airtight container. Makes 1-1/2 pounds.

### Ingredients:

- 1/2 c. butter
- 1/2 c. creamy peanut butter
- 1 c. chocolate chips
- 12-oz. pkg. bite-size crispy rice or corn cereal squares
- 1 lb. powdered sugar

Through all the holiday traditions of decorating the house and tree, baking cookies and buying gifts, we become rushed and stressed. Before we know it, it's Christmas Eve and the big day is finally upon us. This is the time the true joy of the season is felt. Our Christmas Eve traditions start when my husband takes the kids out to "wear them out." I wrap gifts, finish all the baking and make sure the food is ready. When they return, we all enjoy dinner together and attend a candlelight Christmas Eve church service. After church, we drive through the neighborhoods and admire the decorations and lights. Once we're home, we share hot cocoa and sample the cookies for Santa. The stockings are hung on the mantel and, as we snuggle together and drift off to sleep, the true meaning of Christmas is warm in our hearts. These simple traditions are such a joy and pleasure. I know that when the children are grown and off on their own, there will be an emptiness that only grandchildren will be able to fill.

*Judy Haller*
*Dover, DE*

# Blessings

## Seven-Layer Cookies

1/2 c. butter, melted
1-1/2 c. graham cracker
    crumbs
14-oz. can sweetened
    condensed milk

1 c. chocolate chips
1 c. butterscotch chips
1 c. chopped pecans
1-1/3 c. flaked coconut

Place butter in a 13"x9" baking pan; turn to coat bottom. Sprinkle graham cracker crumbs evenly into baking pan, stir to blend with butter; add condensed milk and mix again. Press mixture in bottom of pan; layer chocolate chips, butterscotch chips and pecans over crumb mixture. Lightly press the coconut on top of the layers. Bake at 350 degrees for 30 to 35 minutes or until coconut is golden. Let cool 5 to 10 minutes and cut in bars. Makes about one dozen bars.

Like a lot of mothers, I don't measure ingredients when I bake or cook…it's always been a pinch of this, a scoop of that. One day, my daughter asked me how she was ever going to learn to cook when I didn't write anything down. From that day on, I began to measure ingredients and wrote each recipe down. It took me most of the year but, by Christmas, I had completed her cookbook. I can still see the look of joy on her face as she leafed through it. What a wonderful way to preserve family recipes.

Sally Davis
Payne, OH

# Blessings

## Warm Cinnamon Twists

1 T. sugar

3 t. baking powder

2 c. all-purpose flour

1 t. salt

6 T. shortening

2/3 c. milk

2 T. butter, melted

1/4 c. brown sugar, packed

1 t. cinnamon

Mix together sugar, baking powder, flour, salt, shortening and milk. Roll dough out on a floured surface into an 18-inch circle. Top with melted butter, then sprinkle brown sugar and cinnamon on top. Roll dough jelly roll style and cut in 3/4-inch slices. Place slices on an ungreased baking sheet and bake at 375 degrees for 12 to 15 minutes. Makes 2 dozen.

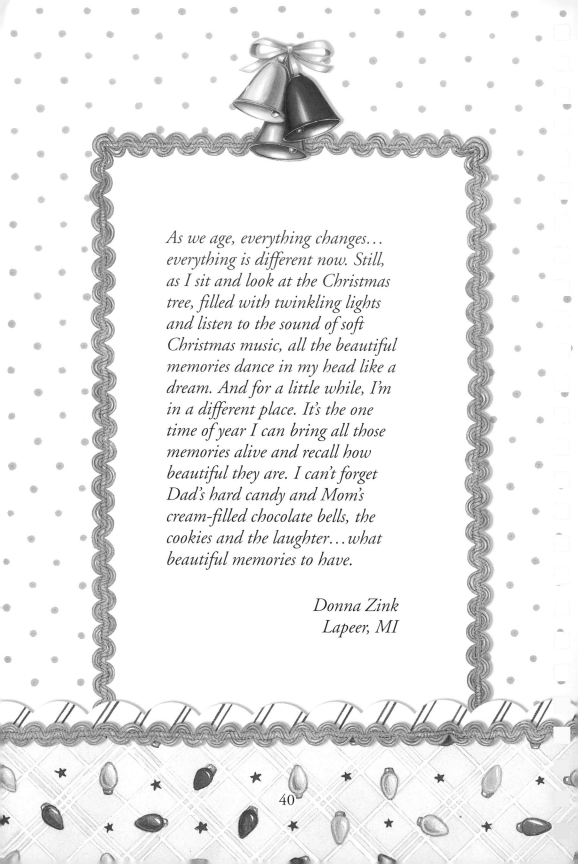

As we age, everything changes…
everything is different now. Still,
as I sit and look at the Christmas
tree, filled with twinkling lights
and listen to the sound of soft
Christmas music, all the beautiful
memories dance in my head like a
dream. And for a little while, I'm
in a different place. It's the one
time of year I can bring all those
memories alive and recall how
beautiful they are. I can't forget
Dad's hard candy and Mom's
cream-filled chocolate bells, the
cookies and the laughter…what
beautiful memories to have.

Donna Zink
Lapeer, MI

# Blessings

## Christmas Cut-Out Cookies

1 c. shortening
1 c. sugar
2 eggs, beaten
1-1/2 t. vanilla extract

2-1/2 c. all-purpose
  flour
1-1/2 t. baking powder
1/2 t. salt

Cream together shortening and sugar; stir in eggs
and vanilla. Add dry ingredients; blend well. Chill
one hour or overnight. Roll out to 1/4-inch
thickness and cut with your favorite cookie cutters;
place on an ungreased baking sheet and bake at
350 degrees for 10 minutes. Cool; frost, if desired.
Makes 3 to 4 dozen.

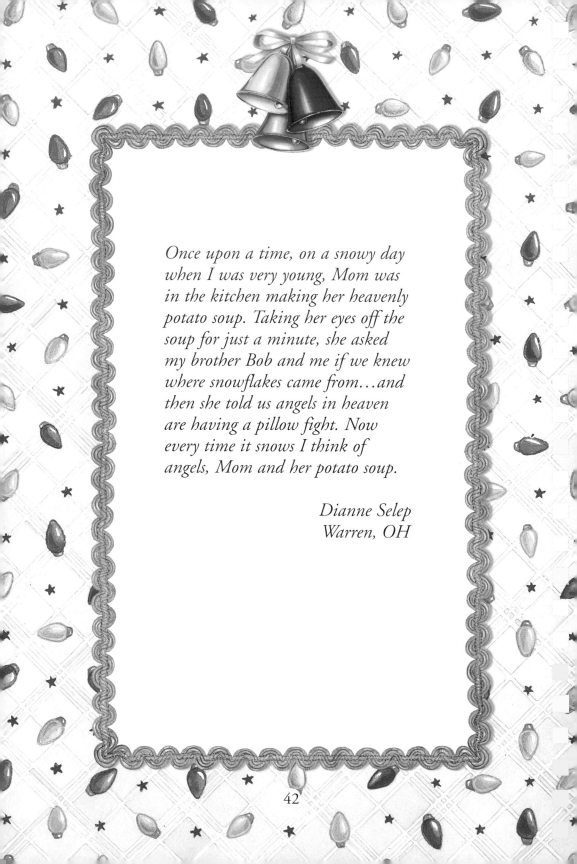

Once upon a time, on a snowy day
when I was very young, Mom was
in the kitchen making her heavenly
potato soup. Taking her eyes off the
soup for just a minute, she asked
my brother Bob and me if we knew
where snowflakes came from…and
then she told us angels in heaven
are having a pillow fight. Now
every time it snows I think of
angels, Mom and her potato soup.

Dianne Selep
Warren, OH

# Blessings

## Heavenly Potato Soup

Place potatoes and onion in a stockpot, sprinkle with salt and add enough water to cover. Bring water to a boil and cook until potatoes are tender; about 20 minutes. Remove from heat, drain water and pour in enough milk to just cover potatoes. Add cheese and butter, then cook over medium heat until cheese has melted. Blend together cornstarch and water until smooth; add to stockpot. Season with salt and pepper to taste and continue to cook until soup has thickened. Makes 6 servings.

### Ingredients:

**5 lbs. potatoes, peeled and cubed**
**1 onion, chopped**
**1/8 t. salt**
**milk**
**4 slices Swiss cheese**
**4 T. butter**
**1/4 c. cornstarch**
**1/2 c. water**
**salt and pepper to taste**

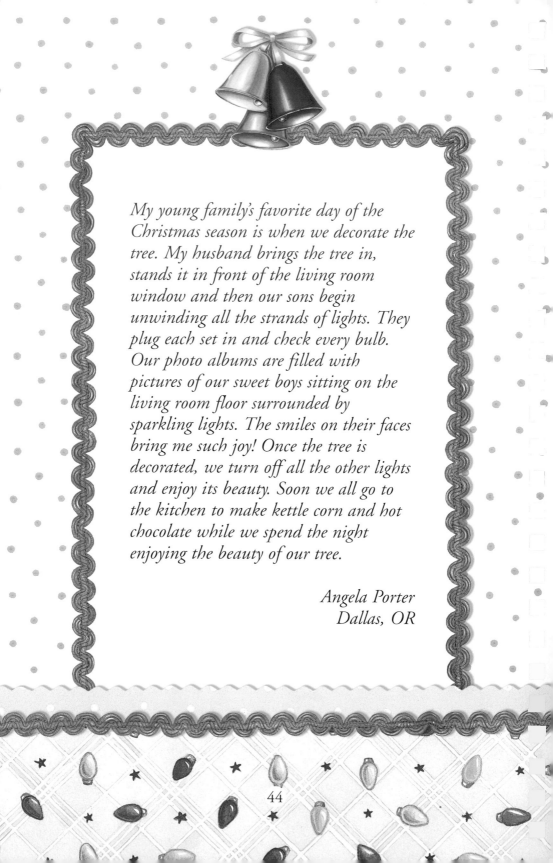

*My young family's favorite day of the Christmas season is when we decorate the tree. My husband brings the tree in, stands it in front of the living room window and then our sons begin unwinding all the strands of lights. They plug each set in and check every bulb. Our photo albums are filled with pictures of our sweet boys sitting on the living room floor surrounded by sparkling lights. The smiles on their faces bring me such joy! Once the tree is decorated, we turn off all the other lights and enjoy its beauty. Soon we all go to the kitchen to make kettle corn and hot chocolate while we spend the night enjoying the beauty of our tree.*

*Angela Porter*
*Dallas, OR*

## Kettle Corn

1/3 c. oil
2 T. butter
3/4 c. popcorn kernels

2 T. sugar
salt to taste

Place all ingredients in a deep pan and cover. Cook over medium-high heat, moving pan back and forth while kernels begin to pop. Once the popping has slowed, remove pan from heat and pour in a large bowl; add salt. Makes 4 quarts.

When Love adorns a home, other ornaments are secondary.

-Unknown

One Christmas, my mom had a special surprise for me. I was excited because it was rare that we did anything without at least one of my five brothers & sisters tagging along. After a hearty meal, Mom whisked me away in our big station wagon. To a 7 year-old, the drive from rural New Jersey to New York City was very long but it was well worth it. We were setting out alone to see...the Rockettes! My dance teacher, Mrs. Thomas had recently mentioned to Mom that I ought to take lessons in the city and I thought my heart would burst! That wasn't possible but instead, my mom gave me this divine treat. What I remember about that day are the twinkling lights at Radio City Music Hall, the hustle & bustle on the street and my small hand held warm and tight in Mom's. Everything seemed to be touched with magic. We waited in line, then in our scratchy seats and finally, they took the stage. I was in heaven! The costumes were fantastic and music filled the entire hall. Best of all, my mom's own face mirrored my own delight.

*Jo Ann*

# Blessings

## Old-Fashioned Kielbasa & Sauerkraut

1 lb. kielbasa, sliced
1 c. onion, sliced
2 t. dried thyme
1 t. pepper
2 c. apple juice or cider
1 c. beef broth
1-1/2 c. sauerkraut, drained

1/4 t. caraway seed
1 Granny Smith apple, peeled, cored and diced
1 lb. red-skinned potatoes, halved and sliced
salt to taste

Brown kielbasa in a large skillet over medium heat, about 3 minutes; add onion, thyme and pepper. Cover and heat about 2 minutes or until onion begins to soften, stirring once; add apple juice or cider, broth, sauerkraut and caraway seed. Mix in apples and potatoes; reduce heat to medium-low. Simmer, covered, until tender, about 20 minutes; salt to taste. Makes 8 to 10 servings.

*I wasn't raised on a farm; however, in 1982, I did fall in love with and marry a farmer. We'd made plans to be with my family one special Christmas and, since we weren't expecting our cows to deliver their calves until early January, the timing was perfect. As events turned out, that year we had one of those Canadian blasts that Midwesterners frequently experience during the winter. The wind chill was down to 50 degrees below zero and the snow was blowing and drifting terribly. When we woke up Christmas morning, we listened to the radio and decided not to venture out on the highways. This was one Christmas we'd stay home. My husband soon went out to do his morning chores and shortly came back to the house and announced we'd had our first calf! The calf was very cold and frost entirely covered his damp body. I quickly gathered old towels and blankets and went to the barn. The cow was gentle and allowed me to get close to her newborn as I rubbed the frost off. We ended up spending most of the day outdoors on that cold, windy Christmas and had a simple dinner of soup and sandwiches. Several times, while we were in the barn with the animals in the silence that surrounded us, we often thought of the very first Christmas when Mary and Joseph were in a stable surrounded by animals. That year, I learned that simple pleasures create the best memories.*

*Barb Pittsford*
*Middletown, IN*

48

# Blessings

## Snowflake Cookies

2 c. sugar
1 c. butter
3 eggs
1 t. nutmeg
1 c. evaporated milk

1 T. vinegar
1 t. baking soda
5 to 6 c. all-purpose
    flour

Cream sugar and butter; add eggs and nutmeg.
In a 2-cup measuring cup, combine milk and
vinegar, then blend in baking soda; mixture will
foam. Alternately, add milk mixture and flour to
egg mixture; dough will be stiff. Roll out on a
well-floured surface to 1/4-inch thickness and
cut with cookie cutters. If desired, cookies can be
rolled thinner for a crisper cookie. Bake at
350 degrees for 8 to 10 minutes or until edges
are lightly browned. Makes 3 to 4 dozen.

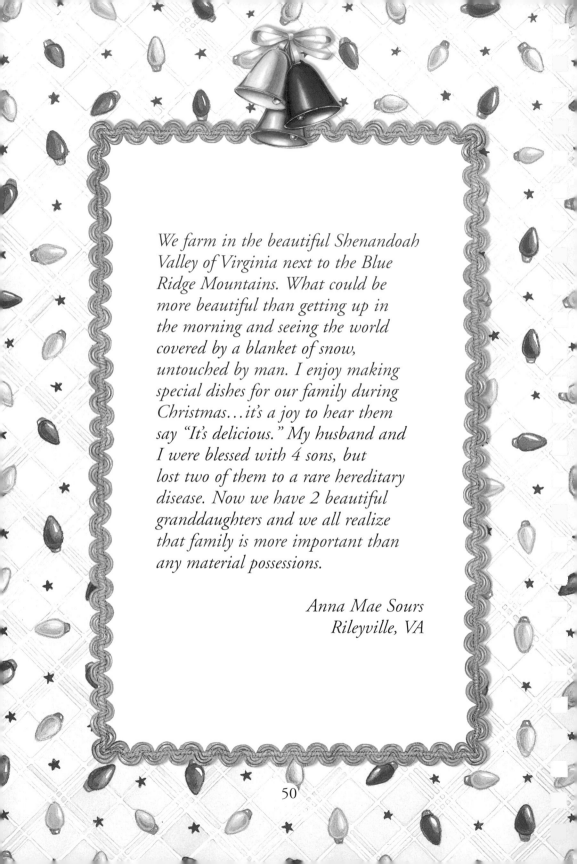

*We farm in the beautiful Shenandoah Valley of Virginia next to the Blue Ridge Mountains. What could be more beautiful than getting up in the morning and seeing the world covered by a blanket of snow, untouched by man. I enjoy making special dishes for our family during Christmas…it's a joy to hear them say "It's delicious." My husband and I were blessed with 4 sons, but lost two of them to a rare hereditary disease. Now we have 2 beautiful granddaughters and we all realize that family is more important than any material possessions.*

*Anna Mae Sours*
*Rileyville, VA*

# Blessings

## Cabbage Casserole

Place cabbage in a large mixing bowl and cover with cold water; refrigerate 30 minutes. Combine 1-1/2 cups cereal with melted butter; press in a 3-quart baking dish. Drain cabbage and spread over cereal; sprinkle with salt. Heat mayonnaise, milk and soup together in a small saucepan and spoon over cabbage. Top with cheese, remaining cereal and dot with butter. Bake at 325 degrees for 35 minutes. Makes 4 to 6 servings.

### Ingredients:

1 to 2 c. cabbage, shredded

2 c. corn flake cereal, crushed and divided

2 T. butter, melted

1/4 t. salt

1/2 c. mayonnaise

1 c. milk

10-3/4 oz. can cream of celery soup

1 c. shredded Cheddar cheese

3 T. butter

*Each year my daughter and I host a Christmas brunch and invite all our friends…young and old! The candles are lit, Christmas carols can be heard softly playing and lights are twinkling on the tree as we sip spiced cider and visit by a crackling fire. We share in a Bible study, then have a gift exchange. Everyone leaves with a gift in hand, a full tummy, warm heart and an eagerness to start the most blessed season of the year.*

*Vicki Lane*
*Valley Center, CA*

Seek not outside
yourself,
Heaven is within.

-Mary Lou Cook

# Blessings

## Pumpkin Coffee Cake

1/2 c. plus 1/3 c. butter, divided
3/4 c. plus 1/3 c. sugar, divided
4 eggs, divided
1 t. vanilla extract
2 c. all-purpose flour
1 t. baking powder
1 t. baking soda
1 c. sour cream
16-oz. can pumpkin
1 t. pumpkin pie spice
1 c. brown sugar, packed
2 t. cinnamon
1 c. chopped nuts

Cream 1/2 cup butter, 3/4 cup sugar and 3 eggs; add vanilla. Mix in flour, baking powder and baking soda. Add sour cream; set batter aside. Stir together pumpkin, remaining egg and sugar, stir in pie spice and set aside. Prepare streusel by combining brown sugar, 1/3 cup butter, cinnamon and nuts; set aside. Spray a 13"x9" baking dish with non-stick vegetable spray and spoon in half the batter, layer on half the streusel, then all pumpkin mixture. Spread on remaining batter, then top with remaining streusel mixture. Bake at 325 degrees for 50 to 60 minutes or until a toothpick inserted in the center comes out clean. Makes 15 servings.

My late mother-in-law, Ida, who was such a loving and giving person, taught and encouraged me to be a better cook. I was a very young "city girl" when I married my husband 35 years ago. I thought I knew how to cook, but Mom King lovingly showed me how to prepare some of my husband's favorite dishes. The first task I needed Mom to interpret was "a pinch of this and a dash of that" into cup measurements. I was not an accomplished enough cook and I needed instructions spelled out on how much of each ingredient I needed to make the recipe taste right. Sweet potato pie is my husband's favorite recipe and I'm so thankful Mom shared it with me. I think of her every time I prepare this pie and how I'm continuing to pass on her legacy to our children and grandchildren.

Jodi King
Friendship, MD

# Blessings

## Granny's Sweet Potato Pie

3 to 4 sweet potatoes
1-1/2 c. sugar
2 eggs
1 t. cinnamon
1 T. vanilla extract

12-oz. can evaporated milk
2 9-inch pie crusts, unbaked

Add sweet potatoes to a large saucepan, cover with water and bring to a boil. Continue to boil potatoes until tender. Drain water and set potatoes aside to cool. When potatoes are cool enough to handle, remove peel and discard. Place potatoes in a large mixing bowl and beat on high speed until smooth. Add sugar, mixing well, then add eggs, cinnamon and vanilla, blending thoroughly after adding each ingredient. Reduce mixer speed to low and add milk. Divide equally between pie crusts and bake at 425 degrees for 30 to 45 minutes. Makes 12 to 16 servings.

# Notes

Delights

Cheery holiday fun...

This year my little boy turned 3 years-old...what a
magical age! I think he "wrote" three letters to
Santa Claus, sent them off in the mail and a
few weeks later, received a letter back from Santa.
He was so overjoyed he slept with the letter for
the next few nights. What joy it brought to him!
Santa is meant to bring joy and hope that dreams
can be fulfilled...I always want to remember
that feeling.

Sarah Ercanbrack
Alpine, UT

58

# Delights

## Sweet Holiday Pecan Loaf

1/2 c. margarine
1/2 c. sugar
2 T. baking cocoa
1 egg, beaten

1 T. vanilla extract
8 oz. vanilla wafers, broken
1/2 c. slivered pecans

Melt margarine in a saucepan, remove from heat and add sugar and cocoa; stir well. Blend in egg and mix again. Place saucepan over medium heat and stir until mixture comes to a boil; remove from heat. Add vanilla, broken wafers and pecans; stir gently. Line a 9"x5" loaf pan with wax paper and spoon mixture inside. Refrigerate until set; slice. Makes 4 servings.

Optimism:
A cheerful frame of mind That enables a tea kettle to sing though in hot water up to its nose.

—Unknown

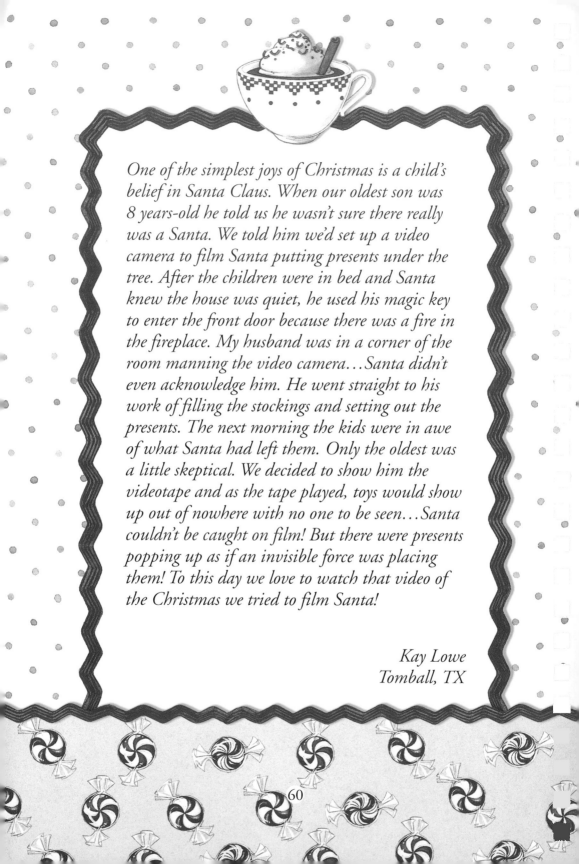

One of the simplest joys of Christmas is a child's belief in Santa Claus. When our oldest son was 8 years-old he told us he wasn't sure there really was a Santa. We told him we'd set up a video camera to film Santa putting presents under the tree. After the children were in bed and Santa knew the house was quiet, he used his magic key to enter the front door because there was a fire in the fireplace. My husband was in a corner of the room manning the video camera…Santa didn't even acknowledge him. He went straight to his work of filling the stockings and setting out the presents. The next morning the kids were in awe of what Santa had left them. Only the oldest was a little skeptical. We decided to show him the videotape and as the tape played, toys would show up out of nowhere with no one to be seen…Santa couldn't be caught on film! But there were presents popping up as if an invisible force was placing them! To this day we love to watch that video of the Christmas we tried to film Santa!

Kay Lowe
Tomball, TX

# Pineapple-Blueberry Salad

3-oz. pkg. raspberry
   gelatin
1 c. boiling water
8-oz. can crushed
   pineapple,
   undrained
21-oz. can blueberry
   pie filling

1-1/2 c. whipped
   topping
8-oz. pkg. cream
   cheese, softened
1/4 c. powdered sugar
Garnish: chopped
   pecans

Blend together gelatin, water, pineapple and pie
filling. Spoon into a 1-1/2 quart serving dish and
chill until firm. Combine whipped topping, cream
cheese and powdered sugar; spread over gelatin
mixture. Sprinkle on pecans. Makes 6 servings.

*My fondest Christmas memory is of a horse-drawn sleigh ride in Michigan. The sleigh held about 30 people, all from different states, and after we climbed on the sleigh, we all snuggled under woolen quilts to keep warm. The snow was about 2-feet deep and as smooth as glass. We started singing Christmas carols, then, about halfway through our journey, the driver stopped the sleigh in the middle of a meadow. He asked all of us to introduce ourselves, then said, "Isn't it amazing how we can all have so much fun and not even know each other?" He was so right…we finished our journey only to realize it would be a moment to remember.*

*Roberta Scheeler*
*Gooseberry Patch*

# Delights

## Coconut Macaroon Cookies

Stir together egg whites and salt; beat until foamy. Gradually add sugar and continue beating until mixture is stiff. Fold in cereal, coconut and vanilla; stir well. Drop by teaspoonfuls on a greased baking sheet; bake at 325 degrees for 20 minutes. Immediately loosen cookies from baking sheet; let cool on baking sheet until firm. Makes 3 dozen cookies.

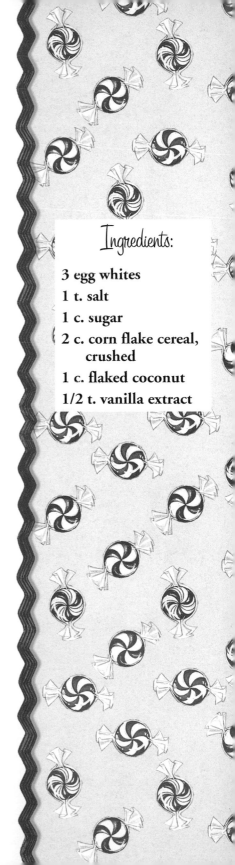

### Ingredients:

**3 egg whites**
**1 t. salt**
**1 c. sugar**
**2 c. corn flake cereal, crushed**
**1 c. flaked coconut**
**1/2 t. vanilla extract**

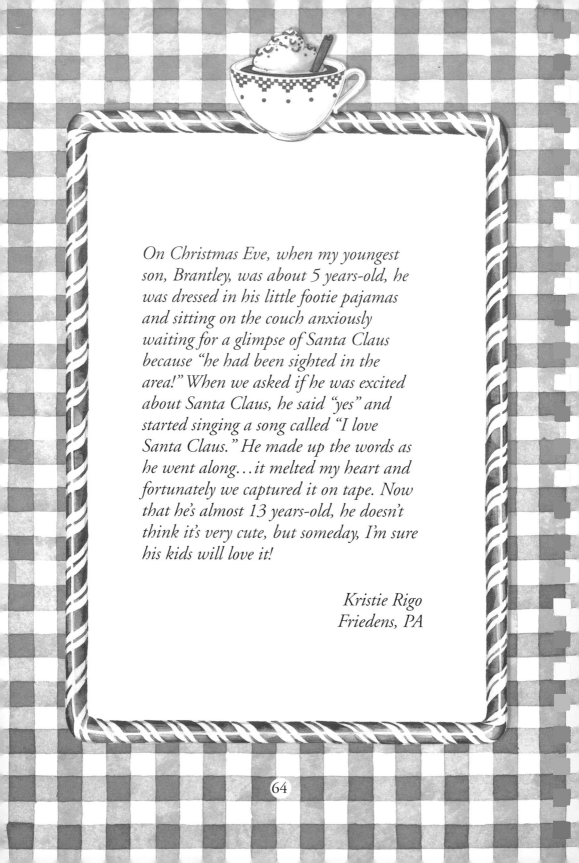

On Christmas Eve, when my youngest son, Brantley, was about 5 years-old, he was dressed in his little footie pajamas and sitting on the couch anxiously waiting for a glimpse of Santa Claus because "he had been sighted in the area!" When we asked if he was excited about Santa Claus, he said "yes" and started singing a song called "I love Santa Claus." He made up the words as he went along…it melted my heart and fortunately we captured it on tape. Now that he's almost 13 years-old, he doesn't think it's very cute, but someday, I'm sure his kids will love it!

Kristie Rigo
Friedens, PA

# Delights

## Homestyle Stuffing

Combine carrot, onion, celery and butter in a saucepan. Sauté over medium heat until vegetables are tender; toss in bread and set aside. Blend soups and water together and add one cup to bread mixture; set aside remaining soup mixture. Salt and pepper bread to taste; stir well. Shape stuffing into 3-inch balls and place in a 13"x9" baking dish. Pour remaining soup mixture over top; bake covered at 350 degrees for 30 to 40 minutes or until heated through. Makes 12 servings.

### Ingredients:

**1 carrot, finely diced**
**1 onion, finely diced**
**2 stalks celery, finely diced**
**1/4 c. butter**
**1 loaf white bread, torn**
**10-3/4 oz. can cream of mushroom soup**
**10-3/4 oz. can cream of chicken soup**
**10-3/4 oz. water**
**salt and pepper to taste**

from Santa

*Every Christmas Grandma would stitch matching flannel pajamas for my 5 cousins and me. Inside each pair would be a little label that said "Handmade with love by Grandma." If she had enough extra fabric, she would make a matching flannel nightgown for herself, too. It felt so wonderful to snuggle with Grandma while we were all cozy in our flannel jammies!*

*Keli Morris*
*Sacramento, CA*

To get the full value of a joy, you must have somebody to divide it with.

—Mark Twain

# Delights

## Broccoli-Wild Rice Soup

Combine rice, rice seasoning packets, chicken broth and water in a stockpot. Bring to a boil and simmer 20 minutes. Add broccoli, carrots and onion; simmer another 20 minutes. Stir in cream cheese cubes and stir until melted. Makes 8 servings.

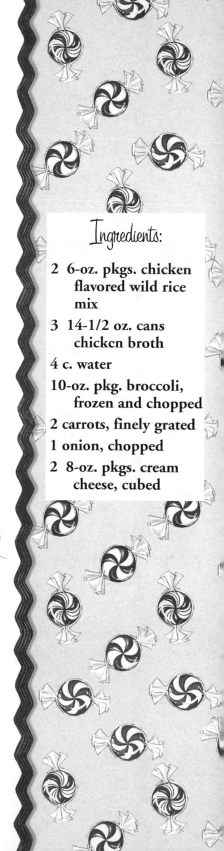

### Ingredients:

- 2 6-oz. pkgs. chicken flavored wild rice mix
- 3 14-1/2 oz. cans chicken broth
- 4 c. water
- 10-oz. pkg. broccoli, frozen and chopped
- 2 carrots, finely grated
- 1 onion, chopped
- 2 8-oz. pkgs. cream cheese, cubed

On a Christmas evening, several years ago, my friend Jackie and I took a ride to enjoy the holiday lights. As we drove through the last neighborhood, Jackie noticed a fresh pine tree that had been tossed out. Maybe someone had a wonderful vacation awaiting them that started early on December 26th, I suggested. She didn't agree. "We must take it home," she stated. I suggested that if she wanted the tree, she would have to drag it to the end of the cul de sac from the open car door, so that absolutely no one would see us! So, there we were, stuffing a pine tree into the trunk of a VW Fox. Off we flew down the street like two thieves in the night, in my opinion, or like two snow fairies saving the day in Jackie's version, no doubt. A case of the giggles set in like never before! We agreed the tree would look great in Jackie's front yard strung with popcorn and cranberries, but she couldn't take it to her house…her husband would think she'd lost it! I agreed to take the tree home and, as we released it from the captivity of the trunk, we were struck by just how terrific the pine smelled. Convincing myself it would be wonderful to have the scent of a fresh tree in the house, I decided it was a real find. With the help of my dear husband, we placed the tree in a bucket of water and tucked it inside a barrel at the end of the hall. We "oohhhed" and "aahhhed" admiring our find. Staring with the amazement of a child, I whispered to my best friend, "Now it's Christmas."

Betty Richer
68    Grand Junction, CO

# Delights

## Gumdrop Cake

1 c. butter
2 c. sugar
2 eggs, beaten
1-1/2 c. unsweetened applesauce
1 t. baking soda
1/4 c. hot water
4 c. all-purpose flour
1 t. nutmeg
1 t. cinnamon
1 t. salt
1 t. vanilla extract
1-1/2 c. golden raisins
1-1/2 lbs. spiced gumdrops
1/2 lb. chopped nuts

Cream together butter and sugar; add eggs and applesauce. Beat mixture well; set aside. Blend baking soda and hot water together; add to butter mixture. Sift together flour, nutmeg, cinnamon and salt; add to creamed mixture. Stir in vanilla; fold in raisins, gumdrops and nuts. Divide mixture equally between 3 greased and floured 8"x4" loaf pans; bake at 250 degrees for 2-1/2 to 3 hours. Makes 24 servings.

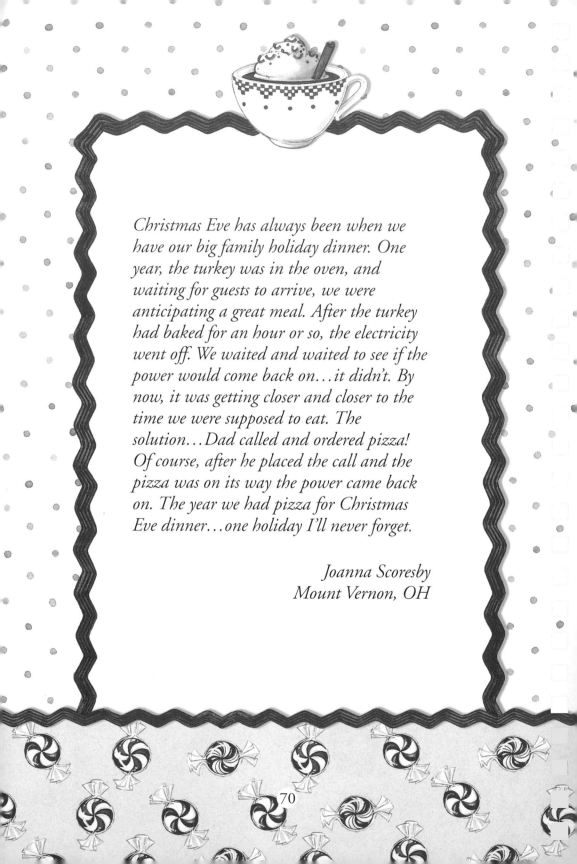

*Christmas Eve has always been when we have our big family holiday dinner. One year, the turkey was in the oven, and waiting for guests to arrive, we were anticipating a great meal. After the turkey had baked for an hour or so, the electricity went off. We waited and waited to see if the power would come back on…it didn't. By now, it was getting closer and closer to the time we were supposed to eat. The solution…Dad called and ordered pizza! Of course, after he placed the call and the pizza was on its way the power came back on. The year we had pizza for Christmas Eve dinner…one holiday I'll never forget.*

*Joanna Scoresby*
*Mount Vernon, OH*

# Pizza Romano

1 c. water
3 T. oil, divided
1-1/2 t. salt
3 c. bread flour
1 T. sugar
2 T. instant yeast
15-oz. can crushed
    tomatoes

1/2 c. grated Romano
    cheese
1 t. dried marjoram
1/8 t. pepper
2 c. sliced mushrooms

Add water, 2 tablespoons oil, salt, bread flour, sugar and yeast to bread machine in the order suggested by the manufacturer; select the dough cycle. When the cycle is complete, remove the dough from the machine and place on a lightly oiled surface. Divide dough in half and shape each into a ball. Roll each ball out to a 12-inch circle, place on an ungreased baking sheet. Form a rim around the dough edge; prick dough with a fork. Let rest 10 minutes then bake at 450 degrees for 8 minutes; let cool. Combine tomatoes, cheese, remaining oil, marjoram and pepper together; stir well. Spread evenly over each crust; top with mushrooms. Bake at 450 degrees for 12 to 14 minutes. Makes 16 servings.

*Christmas cookie baking and eating has been a special joy for our family at Christmastime. When our children were little they loved to put on aprons and stand on chairs to help with the measuring and later the frosting of tree, star and heart-shaped cookies. When they were in college they waited anxiously for the mailman to bring them boxes of chocolate frosted spicy hearts and twisted candy cane cookies. For the past several years, our daughter has enjoyed sharing her baking tradition with co-workers. Since she lives many miles from us now, part of her tradition is to call me at the last minute and ask for her favorite Christmas cookie recipe which she has somehow misplaced at her last all-night Christmas cookie baking. She then arrives at work the next morning laden with plates of mint brownies and candy cane cookies to the delight of her friends. I like to think that I, too am there in spirit measuring out the flour, creaming the butter and enjoying her company.*

*Candy Hannigan*
*Monument, CO*

# Candy Cane Cookies

Cream butter and sugars together; add egg yolks. Stir in extracts and set aside. Combine salt and flour well; mix into dough. Divide dough in 2 equal portions and tint one portion red. Chill dough in separate bowls, covered, for one hour. Remove one tablespoon of dough from each bowl. On a very lightly floured surface, shape each tablespoon of dough by rolling under both hands to form a rope. Place the 2 ropes side-by-side and gently twist together. Carefully bend the top to form a candy cane; continue with remaining dough in each bowl. Place candy canes on an ungreased baking sheet, about one inch apart; bake at 350 degrees for 8 minutes. Do not brown. Makes 3 dozen cookies.

## Ingredients:

1 c. butter, softened
1/2 c. brown sugar, packed
1/4 c. sugar
2 egg yolks
1 t. vanilla extract
1/2 t. peppermint extract
1/4 t. salt
2-1/2 c. all-purpose flour
red food coloring

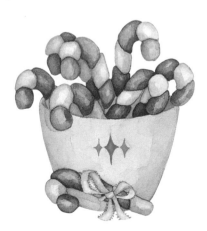

73

*After moving to a new house, my husband and I felt that with all the added expenses, we couldn't be as extravagant with Christmas gifts as in years past. I decided to make most of the gifts myself and went to craft shows, poured over my craft books and set to work. It was like being one of Santa's elves! Our house was buried from one end to the other in felt, jingle bells, beads, ribbons, buttons and a whole assortment of other craft supplies. Our cats, determined to get into the Christmas spirit, would happily dive into piles and proudly trot off with a piece of ribbon or a pom-pom. My husband grumbled about the mess and our poor dog would step gingerly around everything for fear something would jump out at her. Then one day, weeks before Christmas, as I was feeling a little anxious that I might not get it all done in time, it dawned on me that I was having a blast! Because I wasn't caught up in all the usual frantic shopping in crowded malls, I found greater joy in the holiday activities, lights, decorations and music. Seeing the pleasure my humble little gifts brought to family & friends made all the effort worthwhile. It is true that simple joys are the best.*

*Linda Haiby*
*Andover, MN*

# Delights

## Apple Spice Bread

| | |
|---|---|
| 1/2 c. margarine | 1 t. baking soda |
| 3/4 c. sugar | 1/2 t. salt |
| 2 eggs, beaten | 1/4 c. brown sugar, packed |
| 1 c. chunky applesauce | |
| 1 t. vanilla extract | 1/2 c. chopped walnuts, optional |
| 1/2 t. cinnamon | |
| 1/2 t. nutmeg | 1/2 c. dried apples, chopped, optional |
| 2 c. all-purpose flour | |

Cream margarine and sugar; add eggs, applesauce and vanilla. Stir by hand until well blended. Sift together cinnamon, nutmeg, flour, baking soda and salt; add to creamed mixture. Blend in walnuts and apples if desired. Spray the bottom only of a 9"x5" loaf pan with non-stick vegetable spray; spoon in batter. Sprinkle with brown sugar. Bake at 350 degrees for 50 minutes to one hour or until a toothpick inserted in the center comes out clean. Cool bread in pan for one minute before removing. Cool completely before slicing. Makes 8 servings.

I'm originally from California and spent 46 years there. My grandmother was Santa in disguise and my childhood Christmases are full of warm memories of holidays spent with her. As long as I can remember, however, I've always wanted a white Christmas. Each year I waited to hear Bing Crosby's "White Christmas." It just wasn't Christmas until then. It took 51 years and a move to Oklahoma, but this last Christmas, my prayers were answered…my first white Christmas! It was a beautiful one and I couldn't have wished for more…a new country home, a very wonderful and loving husband and a white Christmas. An added bonus, our pond froze and we pretended to ice skate in our tennis shoes! We were so sore the next day, but it didn't matter, to feel like a kid again was worth all the aching muscles. We made snow ice cream the next day and stayed inside, but that was okay, too. I didn't care that I wasn't through shopping, wrapping or baking. All that mattered was the simple joy of my first white Christmas.

Tina Smith
Mounds, OK

# Delights

## Snow Ice Cream

Add cream to a large bowl and whip until soft peaks form. Add sugar and vanilla to taste; mix well. Fold in snow and blend; serve immediately. Makes 4 servings.

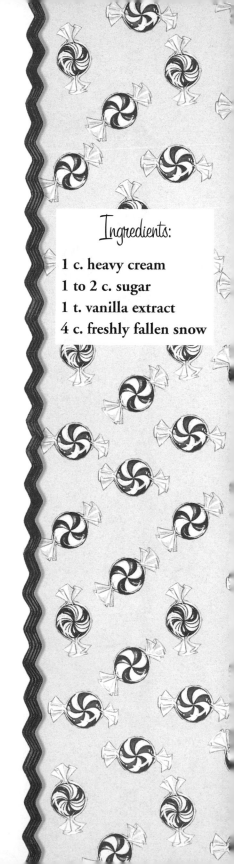

### Ingredients:

**1 c. heavy cream**
**1 to 2 c. sugar**
**1 t. vanilla extract**
**4 c. freshly fallen snow**

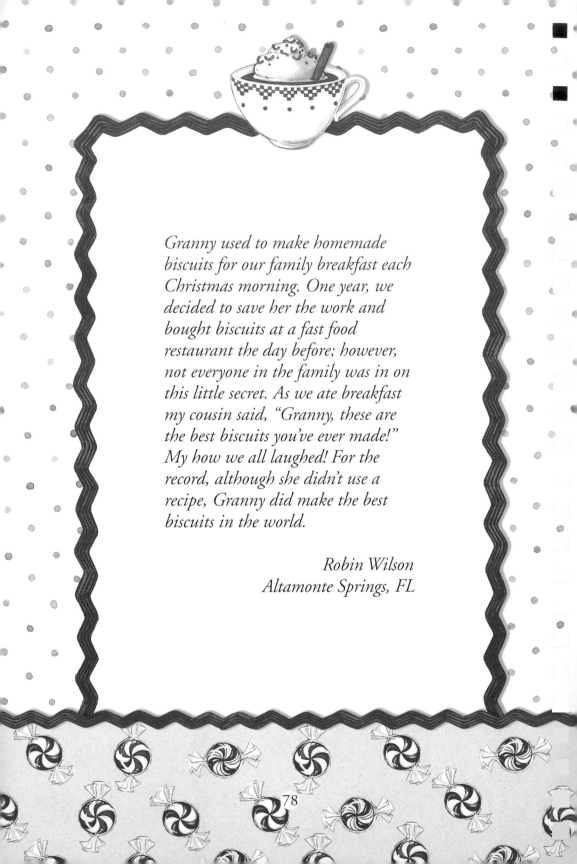

*Granny used to make homemade biscuits for our family breakfast each Christmas morning. One year, we decided to save her the work and bought biscuits at a fast food restaurant the day before; however, not everyone in the family was in on this little secret. As we ate breakfast my cousin said, "Granny, these are the best biscuits you've ever made!" My how we all laughed! For the record, although she didn't use a recipe, Granny did make the best biscuits in the world.*

*Robin Wilson*
*Altamonte Springs, FL*

78

# Delights

## Granny's Biscuits

**3 c. self-rising flour**          **1 c. buttermilk**
**2/3 c. shortening**

Sift flour into a large mixing bowl; make a well in
the center. Add shortening and buttermilk to well.
Work in flour until soft dough forms; roll into
one-inch round balls. Place on a lightly greased
baking pan; flatten slightly. Bake at 450 degrees
for 12 to 15 minutes. Makes one dozen.

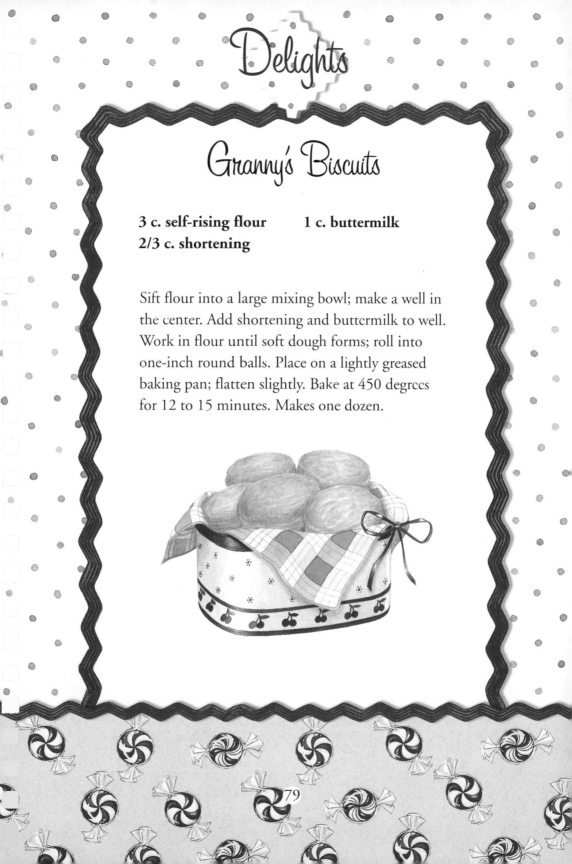

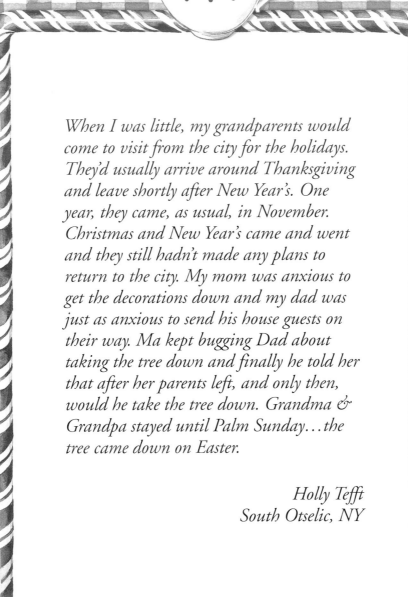

When I was little, my grandparents would come to visit from the city for the holidays. They'd usually arrive around Thanksgiving and leave shortly after New Year's. One year, they came, as usual, in November. Christmas and New Year's came and went and they still hadn't made any plans to return to the city. My mom was anxious to get the decorations down and my dad was just as anxious to send his house guests on their way. Ma kept bugging Dad about taking the tree down and finally he told her that after her parents left, and only then, would he take the tree down. Grandma & Grandpa stayed until Palm Sunday…the tree came down on Easter.

*Holly Tefft*
*South Otselic, NY*

# Delights

## Seven-Layer Casserole

Layer rice, corn, onion, pepper, 8 ounces
tomato sauce, ground beef and remaining
tomato sauce in a 2-quart baking dish. Layer
bacon slices on top. Bake at 350 degrees,
covered, for one hour. Uncover and let bake
10 to 15 minutes longer. Makes 6 to
8 servings.

### Ingredients:

1 c. quick-cooking
   rice, uncooked

15-oz. can corn,
   undrained

1/2 c. onion, chopped

1/2 c. green pepper,
   chopped

2  8-oz. cans tomato
   sauce, divided

1 lb. ground beef

4 to 6 slices bacon

One Christmas Eve, our neighbors asked our son, Nick, if he would dress up as Santa and run through the back yard so their young children could catch a glimpse of him before going to bed. We thought this would be such fun, but our younger son, Zack, still believed in Santa so we had to plan very carefully. I helped Nick get into his Santa outfit while my husband kept Zack occupied. When the time came for Santa to arrive, Nick quietly slipped out of our house. Just as he was running through the neighbor's yard, a window opened and two little heads popped out and said, "Hey Santa, where are your reindeer?" Nick, thinking quickly and in the lowest voice he could muster, said, "They're up on your roof!" He then told the youngsters he knew they'd been good boys, but they needed to go to bed now so he could leave their presents. After they closed the window Nick ran home and quickly changed clothes. While setting out cookies and milk for Santa we heard Nick tell Zack they'd better get to bed soon…that Santa had been spotted in the neighborhood.

Susan Kennedy
Delaware, OH

82

# Delights

## Cookie Jar Gingersnaps

| | |
|---|---|
| 2 c. all-purpose flour | 3/4 c. shortening |
| 1 T. ground ginger | 2 c. sugar, divided |
| 2 t. baking soda | 1 egg |
| 1 t. cinnamon | 1/4 c. molasses |
| 1/2 t. salt | |

Sift together first 5 ingredients. Cream shortening and
one cup sugar gradually until well blended; beat in egg
and molasses. Mix in dry ingredients; form into small
balls and roll in remaining sugar. Place 2 inches apart on
an ungreased baking sheet. Bake in a 350 degree oven for
12 to 15 minutes or until tops are rounded, crackly and
lightly brown. Makes 4 to 5 dozen.

The Seasons may
come and go,
but Friends
last forever.

-Unknown

*A joy of Christmas is celebrating traditions from our heritage. My parents were raised in the Netherlands so our family always celebrated St. Nicholas Day on December 6th. My husband and I continued the tradition with our children…shoes are chosen with care, size and cleanliness are carefully considered and then they're set by the fireplace before going to bed. If the owner of the shoe has been very good, in the morning they will very likely be surprised by a shoe brimming with candy, an orange and a little gift or two. However, if the owner needs a gentle reminder to perhaps help out a bit more willingly with chores, they very well may find a lump of coal instead…along with a few treats, of course, because no one is ever all that bad in St. Nicholas' eye…especially during the holiday season!*

*Carol Burns*
*Gooseberry Patch*

# Delights

## Beef Tenderloin

Rub 2 tablespoons oil over tenderloin; cover and refrigerate one hour. Heat remaining oil; brown meat and remove from pan, reserving juices. Place tenderloin in foiled-lined 13"x9" baking pan; bake, covered, at 450 degrees for 35 to 50 minutes or until meat thermometer reaches 150 degrees. Meanwhile, add onions and broth to reserved juices in a saucepan. Cook over medium heat, stirring constantly until mixture comes to a full boil for 5 minutes. Add butter and pine nuts; stir until butter is melted. Place meat on a platter; sprinkle with almonds, walnuts and blue cheese; serve with warm sauce. Makes 12 servings.

### Ingredients:

- 4 T. oil, divided
- 3-lb. beef tenderloin, trimmed and tied
- 2 T. green onions, sliced
- 1-1/4 c. plus 3 T. beef broth
- 1/4 c. butter, softened
- 2 T. pine nuts, toasted
- 2 T. sliced almonds, toasted
- 2 T. chopped walnuts
- 2 oz. crumbled blue cheese

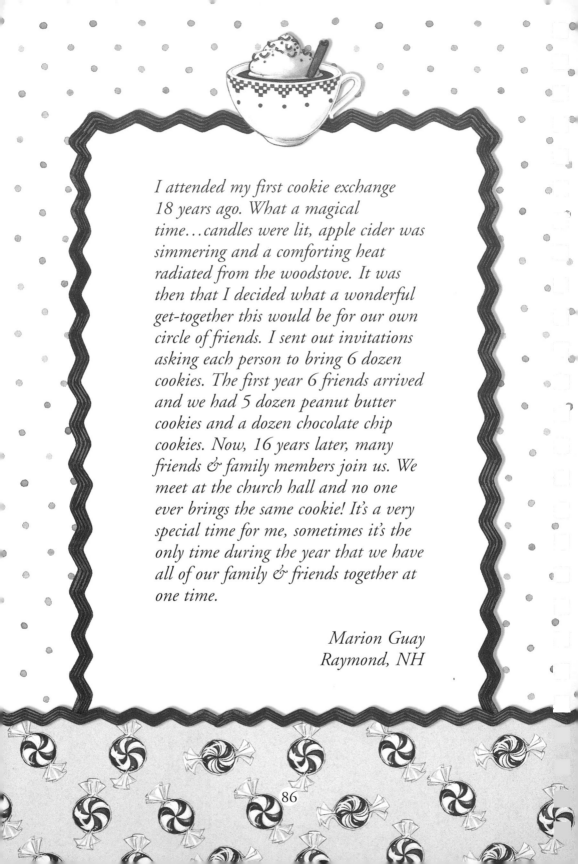

*I attended my first cookie exchange
18 years ago. What a magical
time…candles were lit, apple cider was
simmering and a comforting heat
radiated from the woodstove. It was
then that I decided what a wonderful
get-together this would be for our own
circle of friends. I sent out invitations
asking each person to bring 6 dozen
cookies. The first year 6 friends arrived
and we had 5 dozen peanut butter
cookies and a dozen chocolate chip
cookies. Now, 16 years later, many
friends & family members join us. We
meet at the church hall and no one
ever brings the same cookie! It's a very
special time for me, sometimes it's the
only time during the year that we have
all of our family & friends together at
one time.*

*Marion Guay*
*Raymond, NH*

# Delights

## Orange-Apple Cider

1 gal. apple cider
3 cinnamon sticks
peel of one orange

1/4 t. nutmeg
Garnish: orange slices
    and cinnamon sticks

Place all ingredients in a slow cooker; heat, covered, on high for one hour. Reduce heat to low until cider is heated through; remove orange peel before serving. Garnish each serving with an orange slice and cinnamon stick. Makes about 16 cups.

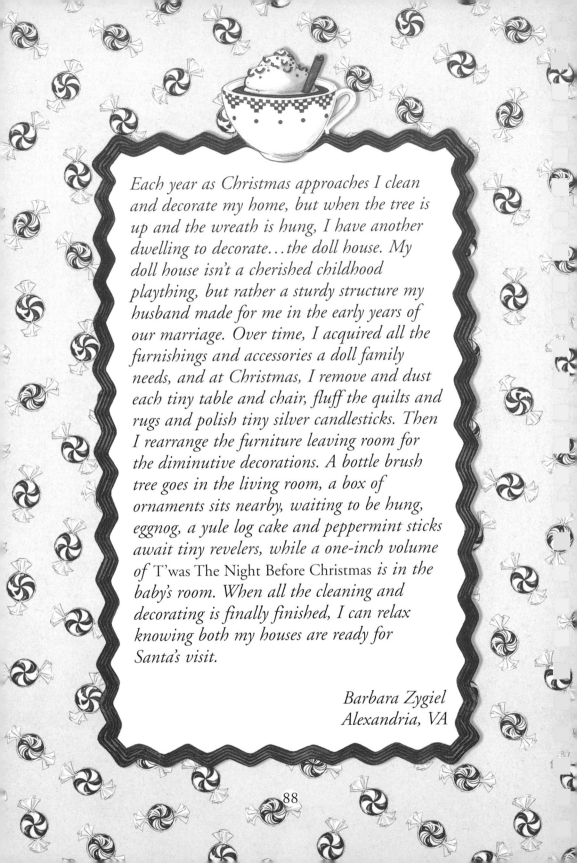

Each year as Christmas approaches I clean and decorate my home, but when the tree is up and the wreath is hung, I have another dwelling to decorate…the doll house. My doll house isn't a cherished childhood plaything, but rather a sturdy structure my husband made for me in the early years of our marriage. Over time, I acquired all the furnishings and accessories a doll family needs, and at Christmas, I remove and dust each tiny table and chair, fluff the quilts and rugs and polish tiny silver candlesticks. Then I rearrange the furniture leaving room for the diminutive decorations. A bottle brush tree goes in the living room, a box of ornaments sits nearby, waiting to be hung, eggnog, a yule log cake and peppermint sticks await tiny revelers, while a one-inch volume of T'was The Night Before Christmas is in the baby's room. When all the cleaning and decorating is finally finished, I can relax knowing both my houses are ready for Santa's visit.

Barbara Zygiel
Alexandria, VA

# Delights

## Cream Cheese Pound Cake

Blend sugar, cream cheese, butter and vanilla on low speed until well blended; add eggs and set aside. Sift flour with baking powder; gradually add to butter mixture. Pour into a greased 9"x5" loaf pan and bake at 325 degrees for one hour and 20 minutes. Cool 5 minutes; remove from pan. Sprinkle with powdered sugar. Makes 8 servings.

### Ingredients:

- 1-1/2 c. sugar
- 8-oz. pkg. cream cheese, softened
- 3/4 c. butter
- 1-1/2 t. vanilla extract
- 4 eggs
- 2 c. cake flour
- 1-1/2 t. baking powder
- Garnish: powdered sugar

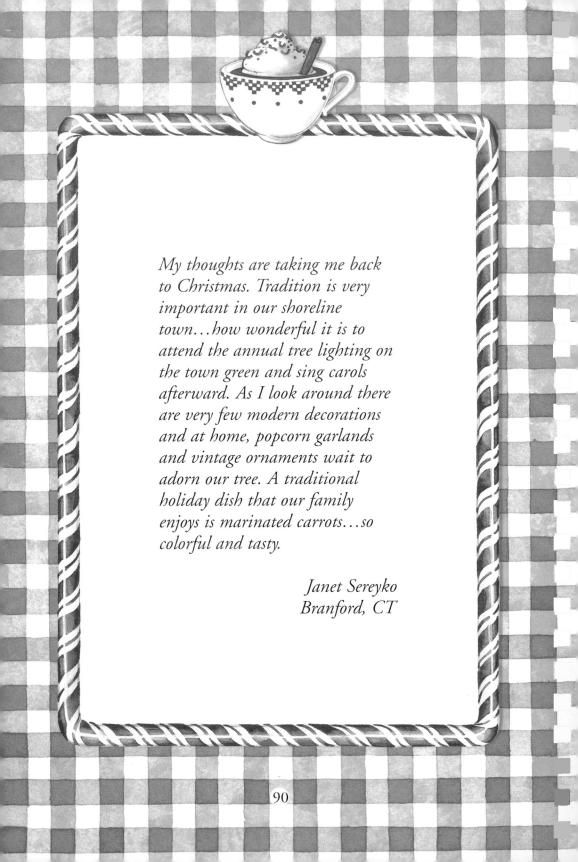

*My thoughts are taking me back to Christmas. Tradition is very important in our shoreline town…how wonderful it is to attend the annual tree lighting on the town green and sing carols afterward. As I look around there are very few modern decorations and at home, popcorn garlands and vintage ornaments wait to adorn our tree. A traditional holiday dish that our family enjoys is marinated carrots…so colorful and tasty.*

*Janet Sereyko*
*Branford, CT*

# Delights

## Marinated Carrots

Place carrots in a saucepan and cover with water. Bring to a boil and boil 5 minutes. Drain and cool slightly. Blend mustard and oil in a mixing bowl; add sugar, pepper, vinegar and soup until well blended. Stir in onion and green pepper, add warm carrots. Cover and chill several hours or overnight. Makes 6 to 8 servings.

### Ingredients:

2 lbs. carrots, pared and sliced

1 t. dry mustard

1/2 c. oil

3/4 c. sugar

1/2 t. pepper

3/4 c. apple cider vinegar

10-3/4 oz. can tomato soup

1 onion, finely chopped

1 green pepper, chopped

*I love being with my daughter and her wonderful husband on Christmas Eve, as well as spending time with my great-grandson, Jason Paul who is 8 months-old. Watching his little face light up when he received his first Christmas gifts and how he loved feeling the colorful wrapping paper in his hands...oh, how we adore him!*

Annette Wesgaites
Hazleton, PA

# Delights

## Family Favorite Lasagna

**2 c. ricotta cheese**
**3 c. shredded mozzarella cheese**
**3/4 c. grated Parmesan cheese, divided**

**2 eggs**
**1 lb. ground beef, browned**
**16-oz. jar spaghetti sauce**
**12 lasagna noodles, cooked**

Combine ricotta, mozzarella, 1/2 cup Parmesan cheese and eggs. Combine ground beef and spaghetti sauce. In 2, 11"x7" baking dishes, layer one cup spaghetti sauce mixture, 2 noodles and 1-1/4 cup of the ricotta mixture. Repeat layers ending with sauce; top with remaining Parmesan. Bake at 400 degrees for 30 minutes; let stand 10 minutes before cutting. Makes 12 servings.

## Nothing is worth more than this day.

-Johann von Goethe

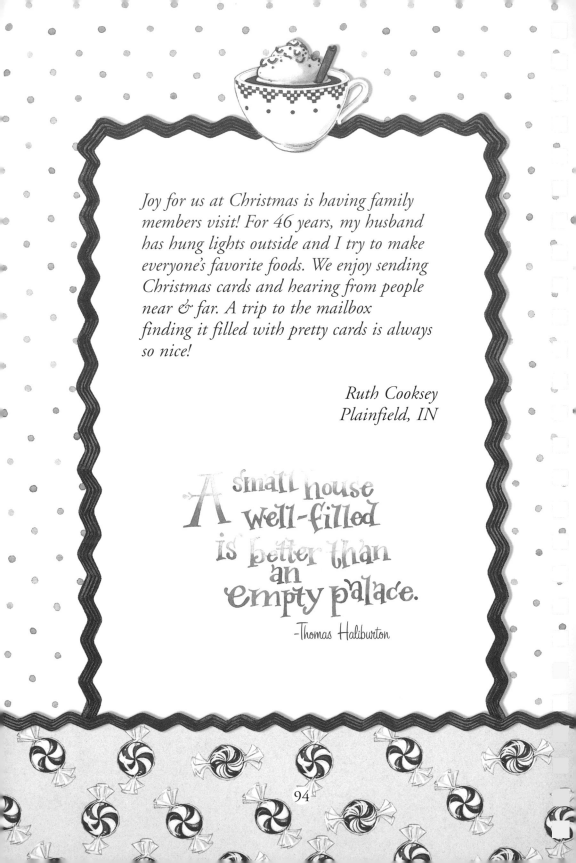

*Joy for us at Christmas is having family members visit! For 46 years, my husband has hung lights outside and I try to make everyone's favorite foods. We enjoy sending Christmas cards and hearing from people near & far. A trip to the mailbox finding it filled with pretty cards is always so nice!*

*Ruth Cooksey*
*Plainfield, IN*

A small house well-filled is better than an empty palace.

-Thomas Haliburton

# Delights

## Grandma Ruth's Cherry Cake

18-1/2 oz. box devil's food
   cake mix
3-oz. pkg. cherry gelatin

1 c. boiling water
21-oz. can cherry pie
   filling

Prepare cake according to package directions; let cool
30 minutes. Use a straw to make holes on top of cake.
Dissolve gelatin in boiling water, then slowly spoon over
cake; spread on pie filling. Ice and keep refrigerated.
Makes 15 servings.

### Icing:

8-oz. carton whipped
   topping
3-oz. box instant vanilla
   pudding

1/2 c. milk

Combine ingredients until smooth; spread over cake.

*As the December mornings turn chilly, a cozy fire in the fireplace sets the mood for winter evenings and I find myself anxiously awaiting the holiday season. I always begin by adding a new Christmas mug to my collection. I then choose a quiet evening to sit down to enjoy cocoa or tea served in my new mug and watch a favorite Christmas movie with my family. I decorate our home slowly, maybe over a few days, sometimes over a couple weeks. This allows me time to enjoy the decorating and each step along the way. I begin setting up my snowman collection, then move on to the kitchen and my tree and our stockings are the last to appear. Our 2 year-old daughter loves to read stories, so I've started a collection of holiday books which we pull out in early November and read together. She's learning about the magic of Christmas this way and, as she grows, I hope she'll look forward to this as much as I do every year.*

*Danielle Graves*
*Wichita, KS*

# Delights

## Creamy Hot Cocoa

Combine chocolate, butter and vanilla in the top of a double boiler; stir until smooth. Gradually add half-and-half; warm thoroughly, but do not boil. Makes 2 servings.

### Ingredients:

2/3 c. chocolate chips
2 t. butter
1/2 t. vanilla extract
2 c. half-and-half

*The simple joys of Christmas won't be set under the Christmas tree…they'll be hiding in your heart. It's such a wonderful season when love comes undisguised in unusual ways. It's a time to reach out and share joy and the true spirit of the season. If things become too hectic and you begin to feel frazzled, then reach out and capture some simple joys of Christmas. Turn off the telephone and computer and watch* It's a Wonderful Life. *Think of the special people who bless your life and are gifts to you each day. Start, or continue a family tradition… sit quietly in the dark with only the lights from the Christmas tree on and reflect on the true meaning of Christmas. Sing carols at home or in the car! Feel the joy that music brings your heart. On Christmas Eve, read the Christmas story and remember why you celebrate Christmas. Give and receive gifts from the heart this season.*

*Margie Allen*
*Jacksonville, FL*

98

# Delights

## Molasses Bread

1 c. sugar
1/2 t. salt
3 T. oil
3 eggs
1/2 c. molasses
2 t. baking soda
2 c. milk

1 T. lemon juice
1-1/2 c. graham flour
1-1/2 c. all-purpose flour
1/2 c. raisins, dates or
    chopped nuts,
    optional

Beat together sugar, salt, oil and eggs until thoroughly mixed. Add molasses and baking soda. Remove one tablespoon milk from measurement; discard. Stir lemon juice into remaining milk. Pour into molasses mixture; add remaining ingredients. Spoon batter into 2, 9"x5" greased loaf pans. Bake at 350 degrees for one hour, or until bread tests done. Makes 16 servings.

99

*Everyone has one great high school friend they'll never forget. My best friend was Cheryl Johnson. Cheryl's mother, Eva, always made a batch of sugar cookies for every holiday…big, soft, cut-out cookies decorated with delicious frosting. Back when I was in school, most high school kids bought the school's tray lunch, but Cheryl generally packed her lunch. She always brought the traditional bologna sandwich, chips, and a piece of fruit…but then there were "the cookies." She'd usually pack extras to share because the kids that bought the tray lunches would try to trade something on their plate for one of Cheryl's cookies. I decided long ago when I became a mom I would start a similar tradition. I have great kitchen photos of the kids when they were little sitting on the counter with a mixing bowl and wooden spoon. I'd whip up a batch of cut-out cookies for every holiday, just the same as Eva Johnson had. Today, we still keep a big basket in the pantry filled with cookie cutters and the tradition has truly become a family affair with my nieces and nephews joining in. My children are much older now; the oldest is 21 and in college, my son's moved away and the "baby" is 15. You really always wonder if your children will keep family traditions and if they truly value what you've tried to instill. Well, I assure you, they do. Maybe they have to move away from home first because now it's my college daughter who calls home to ask, "When are we baking cookies, Mom?"*

*Tina Knotts*
*Gooseberry Patch*

# Delights

## Eva's Soft Sugar Cookies

1 c. sugar
1/2 c. margarine, softened, or shortening
1 egg
2 t. cream of tartar

2-1/2 c. all-purpose flour
1 t. baking soda
1/4 c. milk
1 t. vanilla extract

Cream together sugar, margarine or shortening and egg; set aside. Sift together cream of tartar, flour and baking soda. Stir milk and vanilla into egg mixture; blend in dry ingredients. Roll on a lightly floured surface to 1/4-inch thickness; cut with cookie cutters. Bake at 350 degrees for 8 to 10 minutes or until lightly golden on edges. Cool and frost with your favorite powdered sugar icing, if desired. Makes 3 dozen cookies.

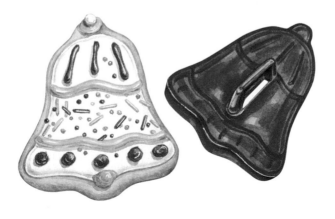

*My daughter, Jessica has always liked being in the kitchen with me even when she was a toddler and had to stand on a chair. Together we always made lots of Christmas goodies to share with family & friends. I didn't realize through the years whenever I got out the big blue bowl she knew we would be having a special treat. To me, the bowl just happened to be the right size for mixing cookies and candy. She recently shared this memory of our special times with me. Now, Jessica is 24 years-old and is a second grade teacher. She lives on her own, and I recently gave her the big blue bowl to carry on the tradition when she marries and has a family. This just shows how we form traditions and special memories with our children in simple and wonderful ways.*

*Phyllis Stout*
*Satsuma, FL*

# Delights

## Oatmeal Surprise Cookies

Cream together butter and sugars; add eggs, vanilla, nutmeg and cinnamon. Stir in flour and blend well. Combine wheat germ and oatmeal; add to creamed mixture. Drop by tablespoonfuls on a lightly greased baking sheet. Bake at 350 degrees for 8 to 9 minutes. Makes 4-1/2 dozen.

Earth's crammed with Heaven.

-Elizabeth Barrett Browning

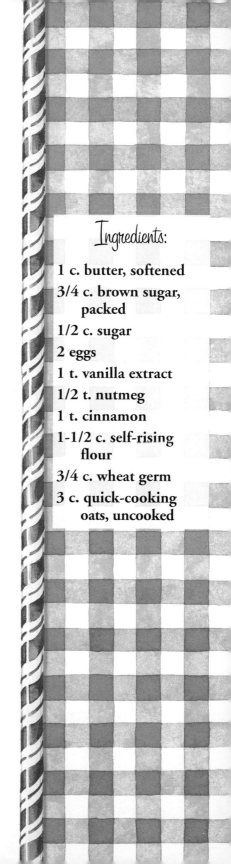

### Ingredients:

1 c. butter, softened

3/4 c. brown sugar, packed

1/2 c. sugar

2 eggs

1 t. vanilla extract

1/2 t. nutmeg

1 t. cinnamon

1-1/2 c. self-rising flour

3/4 c. wheat germ

3 c. quick-cooking oats, uncooked

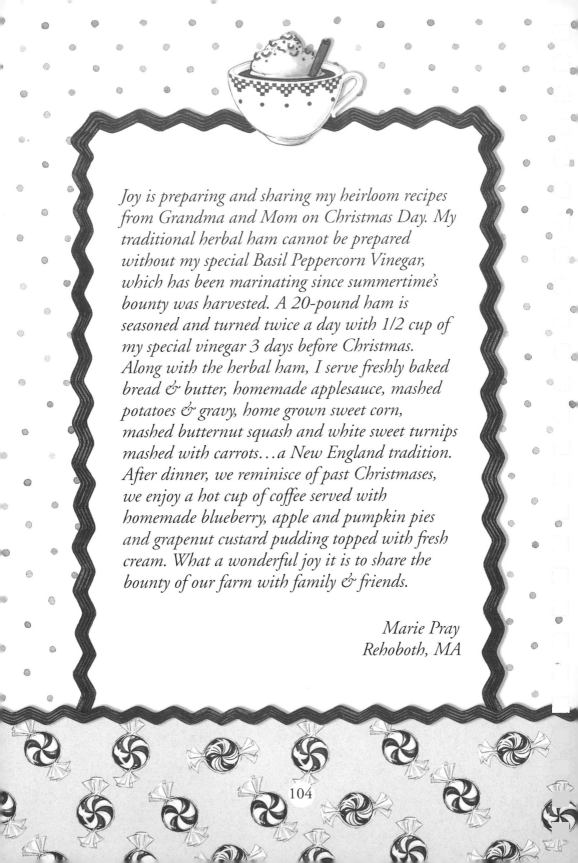

*Joy is preparing and sharing my heirloom recipes from Grandma and Mom on Christmas Day. My traditional herbal ham cannot be prepared without my special Basil Peppercorn Vinegar, which has been marinating since summertime's bounty was harvested. A 20-pound ham is seasoned and turned twice a day with 1/2 cup of my special vinegar 3 days before Christmas. Along with the herbal ham, I serve freshly baked bread & butter, homemade applesauce, mashed potatoes & gravy, home grown sweet corn, mashed butternut squash and white sweet turnips mashed with carrots…a New England tradition. After dinner, we reminisce of past Christmases, we enjoy a hot cup of coffee served with homemade blueberry, apple and pumpkin pies and grapenut custard pudding topped with fresh cream. What a wonderful joy it is to share the bounty of our farm with family & friends.*

*Marie Pray*
*Rehoboth, MA*

# Basil-Peppercorn Vinegar

fresh cinnamon or red
  sweet basil

2 t. black peppercorns,
  divided

1-ltr. bottle white wine
  vinegar

Fill a one-liter bottle half full of freshly picked basil. Add one teaspoon black peppercorns and fill bottle with vinegar. Cover tightly and set in the sun for one month. Add enough fresh basil to a new one-liter bottle to fill it halfway; add remaining peppercorns. Strain vinegar through a coffee filter into the new one-liter bottle. Use as a marinade for meats or tossed salads. Makes one liter.

To prepare ham; combine one cup brown sugar, a drained 20-ounce can of sliced unsweetened pineapple, 2 teaspoons ground cloves, one teaspoon pepper, one tablespoon dry mustard and 1/2 cup basil-peppercorn vinegar. Secure pineapple slices to ham with a toothpick; top with a maraschino cherry. Pour mixture over a 20-pound ham and bake at 325 degrees, basting each hour, for 4 to 5 hours or until a meat thermometer reads 160 degrees. Serves 20.

# Notes

# Memories

## Sweet holiday recollections...

As I close my eyes and reflect on days gone by, I remember the Christmas season, with its blustery nights, when I would find my precious mother in the kitchen making fudge and hearing the sound of dancing popcorn on the stove. My two sisters and I would linger at Mom's side to see which one of us would get the privilege of licking the chocolate off the old wooden spoon…the chocolate aroma in the air, mixed with the scent of popcorn, just made our tiny mouths water for the tasty treats! Our evenings together were magical as we tasted the delights of tempting snacks and it gave Mom & Dad time to hear the three of us tell them our Christmas wishes and dreams. Time is such a fleeting thing. Grab every wonderful moment and each loving memory, then hold them in your heart.

*Thais Menges*
*Three Rivers, MI*

# Mom's Christmas Fudge

3  12-oz. pkgs. semi-
   sweet chocolate
   chips
1/2 lb. margarine
12-oz. can evaporated
   milk

4-1/2 c. sugar
1/4 t. cream of tartar
2 t. vanilla extract

Place chocolate chips and margarine in a large mixing bowl; set aside. Blend together milk, sugar and cream of tartar in a 3-quart saucepan; bring to a boil. Continue to boil for 6 minutes, stirring constantly. Pour mixture into bowl of chocolate chips and add vanilla. Stir until chocolate chips and margarine have melted and are smooth. Spray a 15"x10" baking sheet with non-stick vegetable spray, line with wax paper, then coat wax paper with non-stick vegetable spray. Pour chocolate mixture into baking sheet; set aside until cooled. Chill one hour or until firm. To remove fudge, lift wax paper off of baking sheet; turn out onto a flat surface. Cut in bars, cover with plastic wrap and store in the refrigerator. Makes about 5 pounds.

In 1932, just before my 6th birthday, I wasn't excited about Christmas at all. Mama had died 2 years earlier, her loss still felt, and Grandma had hired Ella to care for my 4 brothers and sisters and me. Anna Jane, my youngest sister, asked if we could decorate a Christmas tree, and I recall one of the boys snapping back that we had no money for a tree and there wouldn't be any presents under it anyway. Ella tried to make things brighter…she sent one of the boys to find her gunny sack filled with fabric scraps. The boys showed little enthusiasm as they went upstairs, but a short time later they dragged the bag of treasured scraps down the steps and into the play room. Ella opened the bag, turned it upside down and the contents spilled on the floor…a beautiful collection of assorted fabrics. "I'll help you make homemade gifts," Ella told us. "I'll teach you to stitch the log cabin design for hot pads, small pillows and whatever else you can think of." We sorted fabrics and separated them in piles and soon we were creating designs; it was such fun! My sister Rosemary pressed the fabric for each of us, and as we stitched the pieces together, Ella praised our efforts and helped correct any mistakes. Ideas began to surface and we were excited to create them! My sister Janie made a doll blanket and the boys made marble bags. A week before Christmas the gifts were wrapped in newspaper comics and tied with yarn with names printed on tags. It was a wonderful, simple Christmas, one I've never forgotten.

*Phyllis Peters*
*Three Rivers, MI*

# Memories

## Peanut Butter Candy

**3 c. white chocolate candy coating**

**4 T. creamy peanut butter**

Place white chocolate candy coating in the top of a double boiler and melt over low heat. Stir in peanut butter until thoroughly melted and blended with candy coating. Remove from heat and pour candy into a buttered 8"x8" baking dish; let cool. Cut into squares and store in an airtight container. Makes about 2 dozen pieces.

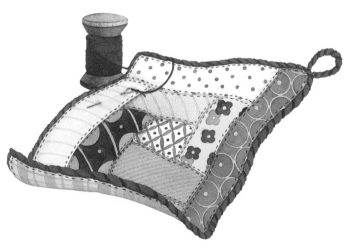

Each Christmas season when my Nana would send me down to the basement to get her box of cookie cutters, I knew I was in for a special treat. Those cookie cutters meant a day of baking, giggling and tasting with Nana and my great-aunt. Over the years we made all kinds of cookies for the holidays and in the process we made lasting memories I relive each time I open that box of cookie cutters. It's a wonderful feeling that such simple things as flour and sugar, combined with my Nana's love, can hold such a special place in my heart.

Cory Braun
Oak Creek, WI

# Memories

## Sugared Jelly Cookies

Sift together flour, sugar and salt; cut in butter with a pastry blender until mixture resembles coarse crumbs. Blend in almonds and vanilla, mixing with fingers until mixture forms a ball of dough. Roll dough out to 1/8-inch thickness on a floured surface; cut with a small cookie cutter. Place on an ungreased baking sheet and bake at 350 degrees for 8 to 10 minutes. While cookies are still hot, turn half of them over and spread the flat side of each with jelly. Top jelly with the flat side of a second cookie; sprinkle with sugar. Makes 6 to 7 dozen.

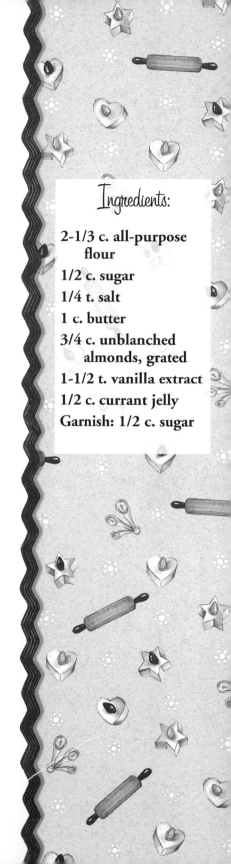

### Ingredients:

2-1/3 c. all-purpose flour
1/2 c. sugar
1/4 t. salt
1 c. butter
3/4 c. unblanched almonds, grated
1-1/2 t. vanilla extract
1/2 c. currant jelly
Garnish: 1/2 c. sugar

Happiness
is not perfected
until
it is shared.

—Jane Porter

*When my parents were married in 1970, they bought a small artificial tree from the local hardware store. It stood about 12 inches high and was decorated with colorful glass balls and tiny twinkling lights. Beneath the tree sat an elf on a pine cone warming himself near a glowing fire. Dad connected the tree to the stereo, so when the stereo was turned on, the tree lit up. All of our other decorations waited until the week before Christmas, but this little tree started the season Thanksgiving night. My favorite memories are of listening to Christmas records and watching that tree sparkle. I was sure that I could feel the heat from that little fire just as the elf did. Thirty years and 5 children later, my parents still put that little tree up on their stereo each Thanksgiving night. Compact discs have replaced the record albums and grandchildren have been added to our family, but my memory of that tree remains.*

*Jody Lenz*
*Dresser, WI*

# Memories

## Cherry Winks

3/4 c. shortening
1 c. sugar
2 eggs
2 T. milk
1 t. vanilla extract
2-1/4 c. all-purpose
   flour

1/2 t. baking soda
1 t. baking powder
1/2 t. salt
2-1/2 c. corn flake
   cereal, crushed
Garnish: maraschino
   cherries, quartered

Blend together shortening, sugar, eggs, milk and vanilla; set aside. Sift together flour, baking soda, baking powder and salt; add to shortening mixture. Shape teaspoonfuls of dough into balls, roll in cereal and top each with a cherry quarter. Place cookies on a greased baking sheet and bake at 375 degrees for 10 to 12 minutes. Makes 3 dozen.

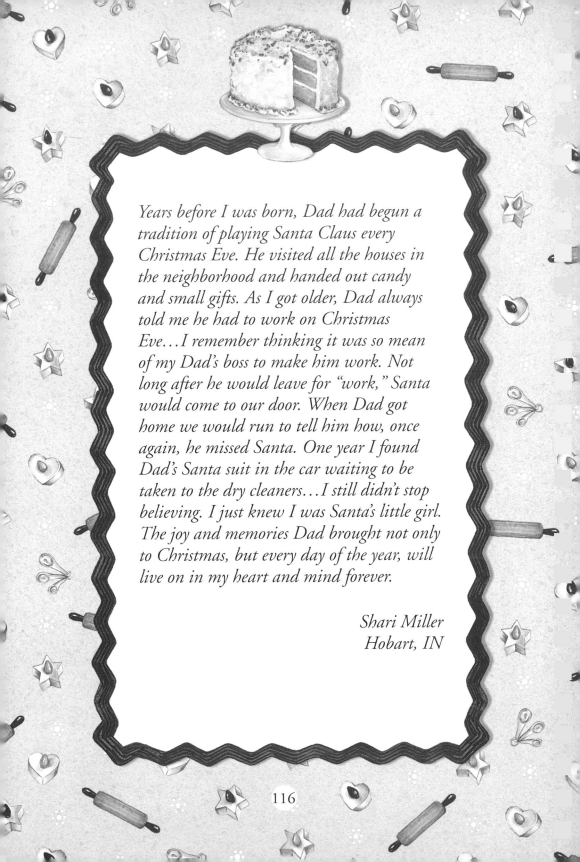

Years before I was born, Dad had begun a tradition of playing Santa Claus every Christmas Eve. He visited all the houses in the neighborhood and handed out candy and small gifts. As I got older, Dad always told me he had to work on Christmas Eve…I remember thinking it was so mean of my Dad's boss to make him work. Not long after he would leave for "work," Santa would come to our door. When Dad got home we would run to tell him how, once again, he missed Santa. One year I found Dad's Santa suit in the car waiting to be taken to the dry cleaners…I still didn't stop believing. I just knew I was Santa's little girl. The joy and memories Dad brought not only to Christmas, but every day of the year, will live on in my heart and mind forever.

*Shari Miller*
*Hobart, IN*

# Memories

## Christmas Cheese Ball Wreath

Blend cream cheese and salad dressing. Add remaining ingredients; mix well and chill. To form wreath, place a drinking glass in center of serving platter. Drop rounded tablespoonfuls of cheese mixture around glass, just touching the edge of the glass. Smooth with a spatula and gently remove the glass. Just before serving, garnish with chopped pimento and parsley. Serve with crackers. Makes 2-1/2 cups.

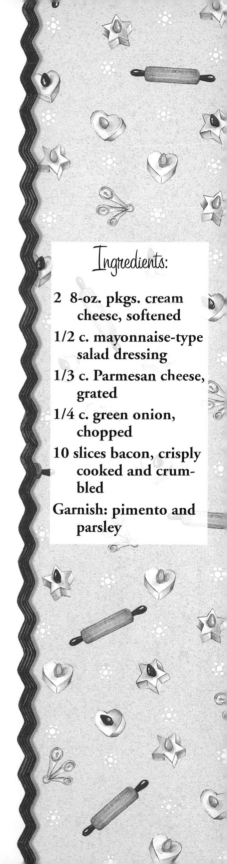

### Ingredients:

- 2  8-oz. pkgs. cream cheese, softened
- 1/2 c. mayonnaise-type salad dressing
- 1/3 c. Parmesan cheese, grated
- 1/4 c. green onion, chopped
- 10 slices bacon, crisply cooked and crumbled
- Garnish: pimento and parsley

*With the approach of the Christmas
season, it is so wonderful to look back
and remember those times when I
was a child. With only a few dollars,
we shopped at the dime store and
always found the perfect gifts for friends
& family. Christmas Eve was spent
decorating the beautiful tree and
enjoying a warm supper. Stockings were
hung and a story read before we were
sent to bed to try and sleep. Morning
meant waiting at the top of the stairs for
my sister…we had to go downstairs
together. The tree would be lit and
whatever was on our wish list would be
there. Life has its ups and downs but
remembering those Christmases of my
youth will forever bring joy to my heart.*

*Ethel Bolton
Vienna, VA*

# Special Spaghetti Sauce

1 lb. ground beef
1 onion, chopped
1 green pepper,
    chopped
1 clove garlic, minced
28-oz. can tomatoes
8-oz. can tomato
    sauce
6-oz. can tomato paste

1 c. water
2 t. salt
1 carrot, finely
    chopped
12-oz. pkg. spaghetti,
    cooked
Garnish: grated
    Parmesan cheese

Brown ground beef, onion, green pepper and garlic together; drain. Add remaining ingredients; cover and simmer 3 hours, stirring occasionally. Sauce will cook down and thicken. Serve over cooked spaghetti and top with Parmesan cheese. Serves 4.

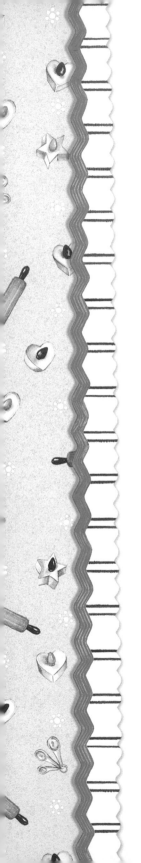

*My Nana was simply one of the sweetest ladies you'd ever want to meet. She made everything special, especially Christmas. Nana's cookies were, without question, the one thing we looked forward to the most during the holidays. The chance to sip tea served in special china cups and nibble her cookies still brings back smiles and tears. I have carried on Nana's cookie baking tradition…all my daughters, now grown, still enjoy decorating cookies with me, and my sister and two brothers count on receiving my baskets of Nana's cookies each year.*

*Gwen Miller*
*Gill, MA*

To love
what you do
and feel that it matters
how could anything
be more Fun?

–Katharine Graham

# Nana's Butter Cookies

3 c. all-purpose flour
1 t. baking powder
1/2 t. salt
1 c. butter, softened

3/4 c. sugar
1 egg
2 T. milk
1-1/2 t. vanilla extract

Sift together flour, baking powder and salt; set aside.
Cream butter and gradually add sugar. Stir in egg,
milk and vanilla; blend in dry ingredients. Divide
dough into thirds and roll out first portion on a
lightly floured surface; cut with cookie cutters. Repeat
with remaining 2 portions of dough. Place cookies on
an ungreased baking sheet and bake at 400 degrees for
5 to 8 minutes or until golden. Makes 4 dozen.

*Jokes about fruitcake may be even more plentiful than recipes for fruitcake! Originators of these jokes must have some of the same memories from childhood that I do...being offered a slice of dark brown cake with unidentifiable contents. My mother's fruitcake; however, was different. The batter was light in color and there was just enough of it to hold together a glistening combination of colorful diced fruit and nuts. She made this cake for as far back as I can remember and following her death in 1985, the huge 12-sided fruitcake pan remained in storage until 1998 when my daughter and I attempted to recreate the memorable cake. We worked as a team that Thanksgiving weekend to successfully produce a cake of which my mother would have been proud. Following my daughter's visit last year, she missed her departing flight. While we returned home to wait for another flight, she said she wanted to do a "project" and we both knew what it would be...once again our special cake was created.*

*Barbara Jo Bunch*
*Marion, VA*

# Memories

## Light Fruitcake

1/2 lb. golden raisins, chopped

1/4 lb. citron, chopped

1/2 lb. candied pineapple, chopped

1/2 lb. candied cherries, chopped

1/8 lb. candied orange peel

1/8 lb. candied lemon peel

1/2 lb. chopped nuts

3 c. all-purpose flour, divided

1 c. shortening

1 c. sugar

5 eggs

1/4 t. salt

2 t. baking powder

1/4 c. brandy

1-1/2 T. vanilla extract

Blend together chopped fruit, orange and lemon peel, nuts and one cup flour; set aside. Cream shortening, gradually add sugar and blend well. Add eggs, one at a time, beating well after each. Sift remaining flour with salt and baking powder; add to shortening mixture alternately with the brandy and vanilla. Fold in the fruit mixture. Grease and flour two 9"x5" loaf pans; line with wax paper and grease and flour again. Spoon in fruitcake batter and bake at 300 degrees for 1-1/2 to 2 hours. Makes 2 loaves.

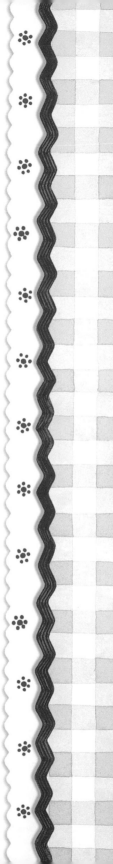

*Holidays during the 1940's were a very special time of childhood joy for me. My fondest memories are of my grandmother Eliza with her steamed English pudding and little mince pies, Mother making sausage stuffing and Aunt Dot mashing the potatoes. All three would "shoo" my father and uncles out of the kitchen as they attempted to sneak pieces of the turkey. My cousins and I would hurry to set the table where we'd gather to enjoy a delicious meal and swap favorite stories of years gone by. Laughter would ring through the house. Now I am in my 60's and they are all gone, but as the holidays near and I begin the preparations for my own family, I feel them all around me. When tears begin to form in my eyes, I find joy in remembering the smiling faces and wonderful aromas in Mom's and Aunt Dot's kitchens and I laugh with my grandchildren. We still never get tired of hearing those old stories.*

*Marilyn Robicheau*
*Farmington, NH*

# Evelyn's Sausage Stuffing

1 c. potatoes, mashed, water reserved

1 loaf bread, dried and cubed

1 lb. sausage, browned, drippings reserved

2 onions, finely chopped

1/2 c. celery, finely chopped

2 eggs, beaten

1-1/2 T. poultry seasoning

fresh parsley to taste, chopped

salt and pepper to taste

Add just enough cooking liquid from potatoes to soften bread; set aside. Sauté onion and celery in one tablespoon sausage drippings until tender; combine with bread. Mix in sausage, eggs, seasonings and mashed potatoes; let stand one hour. If stuffing seems too dry, blend in a little more potato water. Spoon into a 2-quart casserole dish and bake at 350 degrees for one hour. Makes 8 servings.

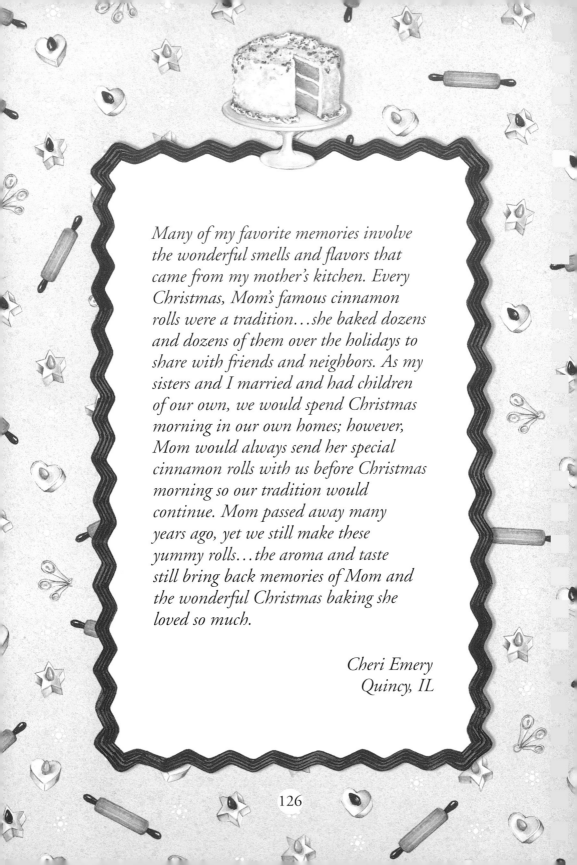

*Many of my favorite memories involve the wonderful smells and flavors that came from my mother's kitchen. Every Christmas, Mom's famous cinnamon rolls were a tradition…she baked dozens and dozens of them over the holidays to share with friends and neighbors. As my sisters and I married and had children of our own, we would spend Christmas morning in our own homes; however, Mom would always send her special cinnamon rolls with us before Christmas morning so our tradition would continue. Mom passed away many years ago, yet we still make these yummy rolls…the aroma and taste still bring back memories of Mom and the wonderful Christmas baking she loved so much.*

*Cheri Emery*
*Quincy, IL*

# Memories

## Mom's Cinnamon Rolls

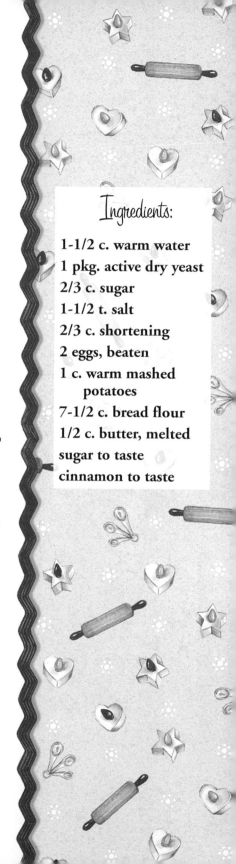

Combine water and yeast; stir until dissolved. Stir in sugar, salt, shortening, eggs and mashed potatoes. Use hands to blend ingredients together; add flour. Turn onto a lightly floured surface and knead until smooth. Place dough in a well-greased bowl, turning to coat. Cover with a damp cloth and refrigerate at least 2 hours or overnight. Remove dough from refrigerator and roll into a large rectangle; brush with enough butter to coat dough, then sprinkle with equal portions of sugar and cinnamon to taste. Roll up dough jelly roll-style, cut in one-inch slices. Place on a greased baking sheet and let rise, covered, 2 hours or until double in size. Bake at 400 degrees for 12 to 15 minutes. Allow to cool; ice if desired. Makes 2 dozen rolls.

### Ingredients:

1-1/2 c. warm water
1 pkg. active dry yeast
2/3 c. sugar
1-1/2 t. salt
2/3 c. shortening
2 eggs, beaten
1 c. warm mashed
   potatoes
7-1/2 c. bread flour
1/2 c. butter, melted
sugar to taste
cinnamon to taste

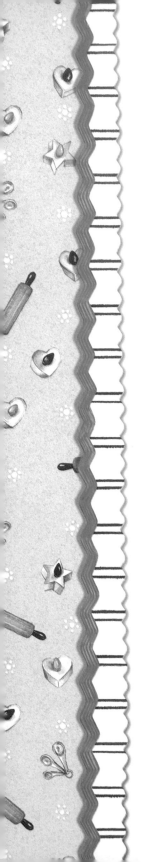

*I have several ornaments from my childhood that all symbolize something special, and as I gently unwrap them each year, I can only smile with delight as I recall how each one was acquired. Because of this, we've started a new family tradition since the birth of our daughter...we give her a Christmas ornament each year. The ornament we buy for our daughter says something about her...from the baby ornament we bought for her first Christmas to the princess we bought this past year because of her love for fairy tales. As she grows, we'll buy new ones to adorn our tree, and when she's on her own, she can lovingly unwrap memories each holiday season the way I have been fortunate enough to do over the years.*

*Meghan Basile*
*Alliance, OH*

# Memories

## Mint Chocolate Chip Cheese Ball

**12-oz. pkg. mini semi-sweet chocolate chips**

**12-oz. pkg. peppermint candies, crushed**

**8-oz. pkg. cream cheese, softened**

**8 oz. chopped pecans**

Blend chocolate chips, peppermint candies and cream cheese together; roll in pecans. Serve with chocolate sugar wafers. Makes 2-1/2 cups.

*Wintertime…frosty, cold December air, a full moon rising and children heading to the lake to ice skate. When the moonlight was obscured by billowy clouds, our parents provided more light from their car headlights which would help us avoid the tufts of grass frozen in the icy surface. Shouts of "Tally Ho!" pierced the crisp night air and a string of skaters would go swirling to a stop. What a wintry treat! Oh, how we wished those nights would never end. After skating until we were nearly frozen, we'd return home with friends and the icing on the cake would be a taffy pull.*

*Maria Kinsella*
*St. Louis, MO*

Take time
for all things.

—Benjamin Franklin

# Memories

## Taffy

| | |
|---|---|
| **2 T. butter** | **1/2 c. corn syrup** |
| **1-1/2 c. sugar** | **1/4 c. water** |
| **1/8 t. salt** | **1/2 t. vanilla extract** |

Spread butter on a large platter; set aside. Mix sugar, salt, corn syrup and water in a saucepan. Bring to a boil and continue cooking until a candy thermometer reaches the hard ball stage, 225 degrees, then stir in vanilla. Pour mixture on prepared platter and let sit until cool enough to handle. Using buttered hands, lift edges and pull candy until it's white and stiff. Pull taffy and shape in a long, 1/2-inch wide rope. Cut into one-inch pieces and wrap each in wax paper. Makes about one pound.

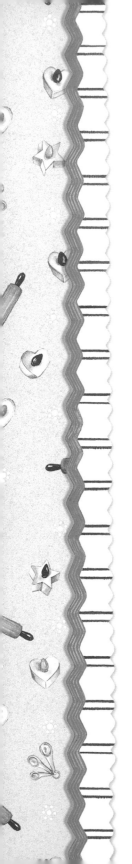

*Several months before Christmas, Dad began building a rabbit hutch. He spent every evening pounding nails, sanding boards, cutting, drilling and looking at plans. Week after week he worked on this project and my sister and I, knowing Dad was always working on some kind of project, didn't pay any more attention to this one than any other. But on Christmas Eve, after my sister and I had gone to bed, I heard a lot of noise in our back yard. I looked out to see my Mom & Dad both working on the rabbit hutch. It had been moved from the garage to the back yard. It was freshly painted and even had a different door on it. The noise went on for what seemed like an eternity, but I guess I finally fell asleep. The next morning, much to our surprise, Dad had built a life-size play house! It had sliding windows with window boxes that were filled with flowers, a Dutch door, a pull down ironing board and even a built-in play stove! I will always be astonished by how Mom & Dad could keep such a big secret and how they worked throughout the night putting all the final touches on the play house. Holiday surprises are so wonderful!*

*Suzie Uhacz*
*Brush Prairie, WA*

# Memories

## Almond Spritz Cookies

1-1/2 c. butter
1 c. sugar
1 egg
1 t. vanilla extract

1/2 t. almond extract
4 c. all-purpose flour
1 t. baking powder

Cream butter and sugar; add egg and extracts. Beat well and set side. Sift together flour and baking powder; gradually add to creamed mixture. Dough will be smooth. Fill a cookie press or pastry bag with dough and form cookies on an ungreased baking sheet. Bake at 400 degrees for 8 minutes. Makes 6 dozen.

We live in a small town in Pennsylvania in a home that's over 100 years old. It has a cozy fireplace, but with a wood-burning stove our children wondered how Santa delivered presents. Because I wanted to keep Christmas exciting and fun for them as long as possible, I began writing notes and pinning them on the Christmas tree. These notes lead to a trail of other notes and finally to the gift that Santa had hidden. However, when our youngest was 7 years-old, she would get up in the night, read the notes and find all of the gifts! About 5 years ago, all three children, now grown, and their families arrived for Christmas. One hour into opening gifts, they suddenly spied a note on the tree and this time the trail ended with a rocker-recliner for all 3 of them! The pleasure that this brought me was more than my heart could hold.

Sue Balfour
Westfield, PA

# Memories

## Molasses Crinkles

Cream together shortening, sugar, egg and molasses. Sift together dry ingredients and fold in raisins. Add dry mixture to molasses mixture, stirring well. Roll dough into walnut-size balls and place on an ungreased baking sheet. Flatten dough slightly with the bottom of a glass dipped in sugar. Bake at 375 degrees for 8 to 10 minutes. Makes 3 dozen cookies.

### Ingredients:

3/4 c. shortening

1 c. brown sugar, packed

1 egg

1/4 c. molasses

2 t. baking soda

1-3/4 c. flour

1/2 c. quick-cooking oats

1/4 t. salt

1/2 t. ground cloves

1 t. cinnamon

1 t. ground ginger

1/2 c. raisins, chopped

I have wonderful childhood memories of Christmas, but the best one is of decorating the tree with my parents. After we had chosen the best pine tree we could find, my father would trim the top and place it in the stand with water. Then we checked the strings of lights to make sure they all worked before placing them on the tree. I remember the sweet smell of my mother's cookies baking in the kitchen while my father and I decorated the tree. No matter how hard I tried, I could never get the tinsel to hang as perfectly as my father did, but he always said I was doing a great job. Every few minutes I would sneak into the kitchen and try to take a few cookies to give us "energy" to continue decorating the tree. My mother would make believe she didn't see me taking the cookies, but then, when there weren't many left, she'd let us know that there must have been a cookie thief around!

Joann McMonagle
Monroe, NY

# Golden Butter Cookies

1 c. butter
1/2 c. sugar
1 t. vanilla extract

1 egg yolk
2 c. all-purpose flour
1/4 t. salt

Cream together butter and sugar until fluffy. Add vanilla and blend well. Add egg yolk and mix thoroughly. Gradually add flour and salt; stir until dough is smooth. Place dough into a cookie press and form cookies on an ungreased baking sheet. Bake at 400 degrees for 5 minutes or until edges are golden brown. When cookies are cool, decorate with icing and top with candied fruit if desired. Makes 2 to 3 dozen.

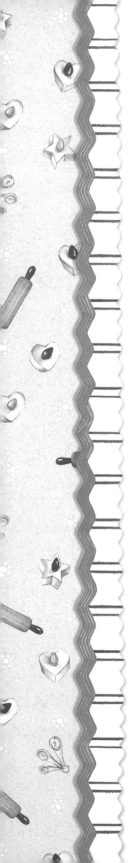

*I'm the 6th generation to have moved into the same farmhouse as my ancestors. When I was a child, my grandfather raised cattle, Corridale sheep and potatoes and my grandmother sold sweet and sour cream, eggs and butter. Growing up, Christmas was such an exciting time for my brothers and me. Nana always started early Christmas morning preparing a large kettle of oyster stew. The old wood stove was stoked until it was hot enough to bake pies and biscuits and Indian pudding would be steaming on top. My stocking was always filled with an orange, toothbrush, toothpaste, candy cane and a comic book. I can still remember the simple joys of those Christmases past and I even use that same old kitchen stove.*

*Pamela Howe*
*Kingfield, ME*

# Memories

## Grandpa Teddy's Sugar Cake

1 c. light cream
1 c. sugar
2 eggs
2 t. baking powder

2 c. all-purpose flour
1/2 t. salt
1 t. vanilla extract

Mix all ingredients until smooth. Divide equally between 2 greased and floured round 9" baking pans. Bake at 350 degrees for 20 to 30 minutes or until center tests done. Makes 16 servings.

*As if it were yesterday, I remember sitting on my father's knee when I was about 6 years old. It was just before Christmas and we had finished decorating the tree. We were expecting company and my mother had set out a bowl of salted peanuts. Dad took one out of the bowl, separated it gently in two and told me that if I looked carefully, one side of the peanut looked like Santa sitting in his sleigh. He was right, I could see him sitting there with his flowing beard! The next time you open a peanut, give it a closer look…you'll see he's still there.*

*Teri Lindquist*
*Gurnee, IL*

# Memories

## Grandma's Fruit Salad

1 egg
2 T. vinegar
2 T. sugar
1 T. butter
16-oz. can pitted white
    Queen Anne
    cherries, drained

16-oz. can pineapple
    chunks, drained
2 oranges, peeled, seeded
    and chopped
2 c. mini marshmallows
1/2 c. whipping cream,
    whipped

Break egg into a small saucepan; add vinegar and sugar.
Cook over medium heat, stirring constantly, until thick
and smooth. Remove from heat, add butter and cool.
Toss fruit and marshmallows together in a large serving
bowl; gently fold in cooled sauce and whipped cream.
Cover and refrigerate overnight. Makes 6 servings.

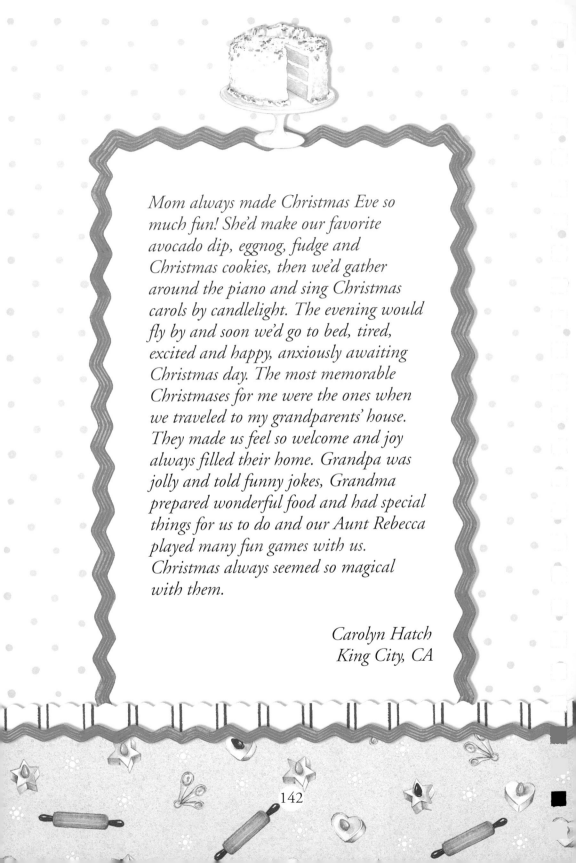

Mom always made Christmas Eve so much fun! She'd make our favorite avocado dip, eggnog, fudge and Christmas cookies, then we'd gather around the piano and sing Christmas carols by candlelight. The evening would fly by and soon we'd go to bed, tired, excited and happy, anxiously awaiting Christmas day. The most memorable Christmases for me were the ones when we traveled to my grandparents' house. They made us feel so welcome and joy always filled their home. Grandpa was jolly and told funny jokes, Grandma prepared wonderful food and had special things for us to do and our Aunt Rebecca played many fun games with us. Christmas always seemed so magical with them.

*Carolyn Hatch*
*King City, CA*

# Avocado Dip

2 avocados, peeled, halved and pitted
2 T. lemon juice
1/2 t. seasoned salt

1/4 t. garlic salt
1/4 c. salsa
5 slices bacon, crisply cooked and crumbled

Mash avocados with lemon juice, seasoned salt, garlic powder and salsa; cover and refrigerate. Before serving, stir in all but one tablespoonful of bacon; sprinkle remaining bacon on top. Makes 2 cups.

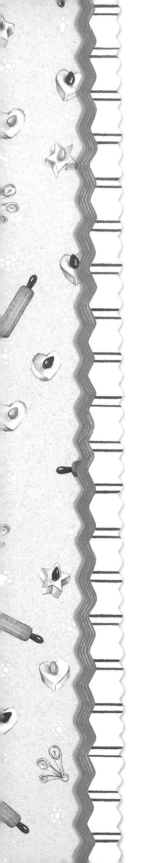

*When I was growing up we didn't have a lot of money, but my parents always taught us to share whatever we had with others. As I saw my mother cook from scratch, I learned a love for cooking that today I share with family & friends. One of my family's favorite recipes is sugar cream pie. It's always a must at holiday meals…as well as a treat in between holidays! Some of our grandchildren live out of state, but when they know they're coming home to visit, there's a gentle reminder to please make sugar cream pie. It's such fun to see they still look forward to enjoying it.*

*Sue Smith*
*Greentown, IN*

144

# Memories

## Sugar Cream Pie

1 c. sugar
4 T. all-purpose flour
1/3 c. half-and-half
1 c. whipping cream
2 T. butter

9-inch pie crust, unbaked
cinnamon and nutmeg to taste

Combine sugar and flour; stir in half-and-half, mixing well. Add whipping cream, stirring until thoroughly blended; set aside. Slice butter thinly and place in the bottom of pie crust; top with sugar mixture. Sprinkle pie with cinnamon and nutmeg. Bake at 350 degrees for 10 minutes; then gently stir filling. Continue baking an additional 30 to 35 minutes. Makes 6 to 8 servings.

God has given us our memories, that we might have roses in December.

—J.M. Barrie

My grandmother always included a baked good with her Christmas gifts to her grandchildren…pies, cookies and candies, whichever treat was our favorite. As we grew up, we soon realized the real joy we received each Christmas came from those goodies she made. Last Christmas there were no homemade baked goods…we lost Nana to cancer. I'm so grateful she shared her recipes with me and that I have them to enjoy for many years to come.

Carol Steinman
Cumberland, ME

# Memories

## Nana's Orange Balls

Mix all ingredients together, then form into walnut-size balls. Roll in powdered sugar and store in an airtight container. Makes 6 dozen.

*Our family tradition for 25 years was Grandpa's "fish pond." Each Christmas my husband, Jack, would choose special gifts for our three daughters and their families. We'd then hang a sheet in the doorway between two rooms and each family member "fished" several times using a fishing pole with a pillowcase attached to the end. Everyone always looked forward to their catch and as Christmas drew closer, our family would start asking, "When are we going to have the fish pond?" In later years, the children even had a fish pond for us...what joy and fun we had. Grandpa Jack is gone now, so the sheet and the fishing pole have been tucked away. Our 25-year family tradition is now a precious memory.*

*Rosie Vickery*
*Union City, IN*

# Grandma Vickery's Caramels

1/2 lb. butter
2 c. brown sugar,
    packed

1 c. corn syrup
14-oz. can sweetened
    condensed milk

Melt butter in a large saucepan; add brown sugar, corn syrup and milk. Cook over medium heat, stirring constantly for 30 to 40 minutes until mixture reaches the soft ball stage, 234 degrees on a candy thermometer. Pour mixture into a buttered 9"x9" baking dish and let cool. Remove caramels from baking dish, cut into squares and wrap each in wax paper. Makes 1-1/2 pounds.

for you!

*Our family loved making divinity every Christmas. Sometimes we made it daily just to be sure there was enough for the newspaper boy, mail carrier, relatives, friends, co-workers and our lunch boxes. We'd keep the house chilly as the snow was falling outside…if the house was too warm, the divinity wouldn't set up properly. As my two sisters and I eventually married or moved away, we still made divinity with our mother whenever possible. My arms would be so tired from patting, pulling and mixing, but never did I hear Mom complain of taking over that big task. She would always say, "Make the house colder and the divinity will change texture." I feel so blessed to have such fond memories of the holidays and I hope, with Mom's help, to carry on the family tradition for years to come.*

*Tina Kutchman*
*Johnstown, PA*

## Divinity

2 egg whites, stiffly
   beaten
1 t. vanilla extract
3 c. sugar
1 c. corn syrup

1 c. water
2 drops food coloring,
   optional
1/4 c. chopped
   walnuts, optional

Blend egg whites and vanilla; set aside. Combine sugar, corn syrup and water in a saucepan. Stir to dissolve sugar, then bring to a boil. Continue to boil until mixture reaches the hard crack stage, 295 degrees on a candy thermometer. Remove from heat and pour in a thin stream over egg whites. Continue to beat until mixture stands in peaks; add food coloring, if desired. Beat with a wooden spoon until candy is dull in color and holds its shape when dropped onto wax paper. Working very quickly, drop candy onto wax paper by tablespoonfuls and top with nuts, if desired. Makes 2 pounds.

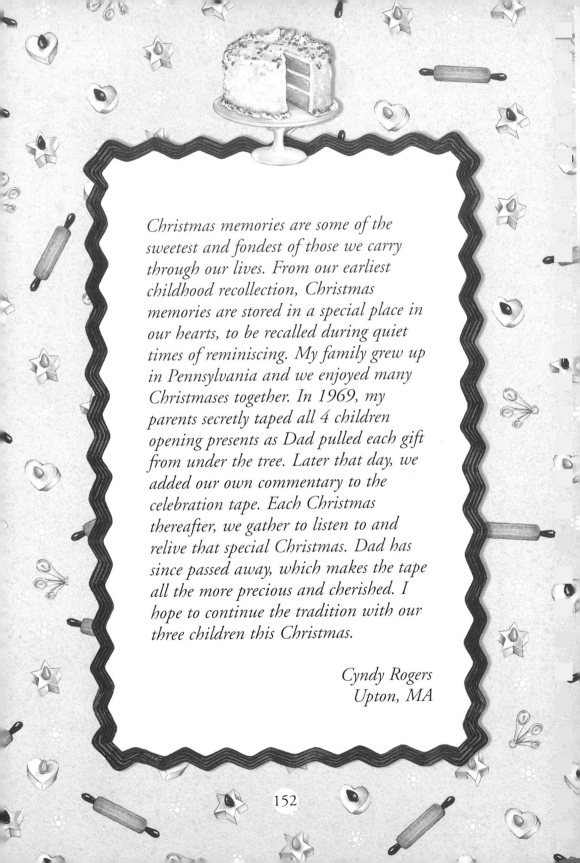

*Christmas memories are some of the sweetest and fondest of those we carry through our lives. From our earliest childhood recollection, Christmas memories are stored in a special place in our hearts, to be recalled during quiet times of reminiscing. My family grew up in Pennsylvania and we enjoyed many Christmases together. In 1969, my parents secretly taped all 4 children opening presents as Dad pulled each gift from under the tree. Later that day, we added our own commentary to the celebration tape. Each Christmas thereafter, we gather to listen to and relive that special Christmas. Dad has since passed away, which makes the tape all the more precious and cherished. I hope to continue the tradition with our three children this Christmas.*

*Cyndy Rogers*
*Upton, MA*

# Garden Vegetable Soup

Sauté carrot, onion and garlic 5 minutes in a large saucepan sprayed with non-stick vegetable spray. Add remaining ingredients and bring to a boil. Lower heat and simmer, covered, 15 minutes or until beans are tender. Makes 4 servings.

## Ingredients:

2/3 c. carrot, sliced
1/2 c. onion, diced
2 cloves garlic, minced
3 c. vegetable broth
1-1/2 c. cabbage, chopped
1/2 c. frozen green beans
1 T. catsup
1 T. Italian seasoning

153

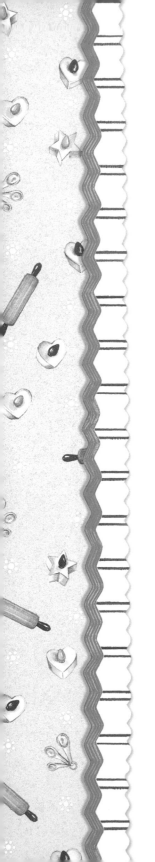

*Growing up, our family made cranberry relish every holiday season. Now the torch has been passed to me and, although originally we'd grind all the cranberries with an old-fashioned hand crank, I use a food processor today. Every year after I've loaded the berries in the food processor and before I press the "on" switch, I think back to when we were kids and the same task was at hand. It took so much time to grind the berries, but we had such fun! With all the holiday hustle & bustle, sometimes we lose sight of the simple pleasures. It's truly those moments, when you pause and look back, that make the holidays sparkle.*

*Lisa Hill*
*Remsen, NY*

# Mom's Cranberry Relish

6-oz. pkg. raspberry
  gelatin
2 c. sugar
2 c. hot water
1 c. cold water or
  pineapple juice

16-oz. pkg. cranberries
6 apples, peeled and
  cored
20-oz. can crushed
  pineapple, drained

Dissolve gelatin and sugar in hot water. Add cold water
or pineapple juice, stir and set aside. Grind cranberries
and apples, a little at a time, in a food processor; place
in a large serving bowl. Add pineapple and gelatin
mixture; refrigerate 4 to 6 hours before serving. Makes
16 servings.

Nobody has ever measured, not even poets, how much the Heart can hold.

-Zelda Fitzgerald

*I will always remember the times I spent the night at Grandma's house. We usually arrived about dinner time...Grandma was the best cook and the aroma coming from the kitchen was heavenly! Along with a roast flavored with her brother's homemade wine, she would make spaetzle, creamed potatoes or green beans and carrots...fresh warm rolls from the bakery complemented her dinner. When it was time for bed, we slept in cool rooms with large feather quilts on each bed and pillowcases edged with tatting or crewel decorating. When Grandma came to live with my mother, those pretty pillow cases were taken to a lady who made dolls. Each pillowcase became a gown for a doll with the beautiful stitching at the bottom of the dress. The dolls were then given to each grandchild the following Christmas. Today, the doll sits in my living room where it always reminds me of spending the night, snuggled in bed, at Grandma's house.*

*Paul Gaulke*
*Gooseberry Patch*

# Memories

## Creamed Potatoes

2 T. butter, melted
2 T. all-purpose flour
1/8 t. mace
1-1/4 t. salt
1/4 t. pepper

2 c. milk
1/8 t. lemon juice
6 potatoes, cooked
  and cubed

Blend butter, flour, mace, salt and pepper together. Add milk; heat, stirring constantly, until thickened. Stir in lemon juice and potatoes; heat until potatoes are warmed. Serves 6.

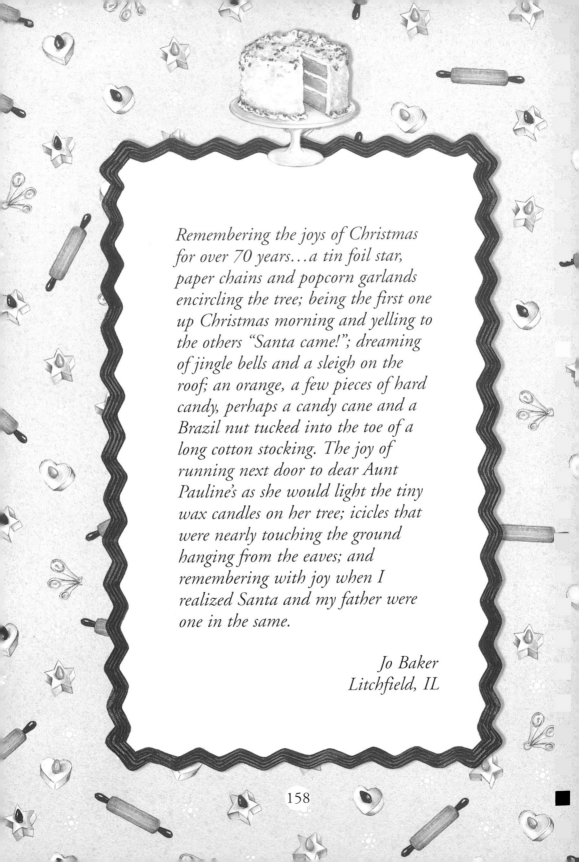

*Remembering the joys of Christmas for over 70 years…a tin foil star, paper chains and popcorn garlands encircling the tree; being the first one up Christmas morning and yelling to the others "Santa came!"; dreaming of jingle bells and a sleigh on the roof; an orange, a few pieces of hard candy, perhaps a candy cane and a Brazil nut tucked into the toe of a long cotton stocking. The joy of running next door to dear Aunt Pauline's as she would light the tiny wax candles on her tree; icicles that were nearly touching the ground hanging from the eaves; and remembering with joy when I realized Santa and my father were one in the same.*

*Jo Baker*
*Litchfield, IL*

# Memories

## Pear Compote

Combine cinnamon, sugar and water in a medium saucepan; bring to a simmer. Add pears and raisins; cook for 10 minutes or until soft. Spoon pears and sauce into a 2-quart serving bowl, thcn sprinkle with chopped nuts. Makes 8 servings.

### Ingredients:

1 t. cinnamon
4 T. sugar
1-1/2 c. water
2 lbs. pears, peeled, cored and sliced
1/2 c. golden raisins
Garnish: 1/4 c. chopped walnuts

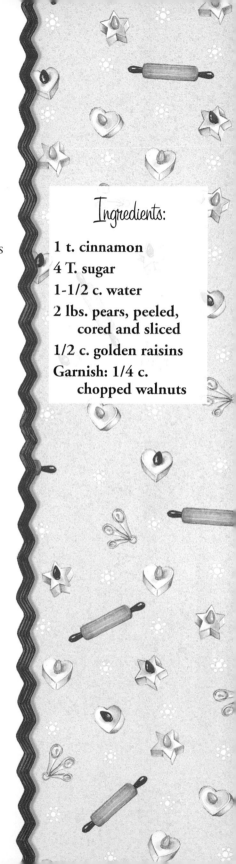

*The year was 1958...I was broke, just starting my first full-time job and I needed a wristwatch badly. Dad loaned me $40 to buy a nice watch with the understanding that I would pay him back. Each time I got a paycheck, I mailed Dad $5 in the form of a check. When Christmas day arrived, I received a nicely wrapped package from Dad...inside were my uncashed checks. Dad had wanted to give me the watch originally, but he knew I needed a lesson in money management. I will always remember that wonderful gift and the love that went with it.*

*Flo Burtnett*
*Gage, OK*

160

# Memories

## Bread in a Jar

3 c. sugar

1 c. oil

4 eggs

2 c. sweet potatoes, cooked
and mashed

2/3 c. water

3-1/2 c. all-purpose flour

1 t. salt

1/2 t. baking powder

2 t. baking soda

1-1/2 t. cinnamon

1 t. ground cloves

1-1/2 t. allspice

1-1/2 c. golden raisins

1-1/2 c. chopped pecans

Thoroughly wash and rinse 8, wide-mouth, one-pint jars in hot water; let dry. Grease inside of jars with shortening; set aside. Fill a saucepan with water, bring to a boil, then turn off heat. When water is no longer boiling, add jar lids and rings; leave in hot water until ready to use. Using a heavy-duty mixer, blend sugar and oil; add eggs. Beat well, then add mashed potatoes and water; set aside. Sift together flour, salt, baking powder, baking soda, cinnamon, cloves and allspice; add to sweet potato mixture. Continue to mix on low speed until well blended; fold in raisins and pecans. Pour one cup plus one tablespoon batter into each jar. Remove any batter which might be on the edge of the jar; repeat with remaining batter. Place filled jars on a baking sheet and bake at 325 degrees for 45 to 55 minutes or until centers test done. If bread has risen above the jar's top, cut off excess. Wipe edge of each jar clean, add lid, tighten down with ring and set aside. As jars cool you will hear them "ping" as the lids seal. Once all jars have sealed, turn them upside down to cool completely. Makes 8 servings.

*As a kid, it just wouldn't have been Christmas without chocolate fudge! My mom had only one cookbook,* The Household Searchlight Recipe Book ©1940, *and this was the recipe we always made together. We made it so many times, I memorized the page it was on…72. To this day, there are still remnants of fudge on that page. We laughed and we agonized over that fudge! We didn't have a candy thermometer, so it was my responsibility to make sure it reached the "soft ball" stage. I prepared several cups of icy cold water (anticipating several "tests"). Once the fudge started boiling, I spooned a small amount of the creamy confection into the first cup…and I repeated the process as many times as necessary (sometimes a half dozen or more!) until a soft ball of fudge could be formed. There were times when the anticipation was so great I cut the "soft ball" process short and, as a result, we poured the "fudge" over ice cream or pulled it like taffy or caramel. It was never wasted though. The best part…I always got the pan and spoon to "clean up" at the end. Thanks for all the sweet memories, Mom!*

*Vickie & her mom,*
*Loretta Nichols*

# Memories

## Chocolatey Fudge

2 c. sugar
2/3 c. milk
2 T. butter
1/8 t. salt

2 sqs. unsweetened choco-
late, grated or 6 T.
baking cocoa
1 t. vanilla extract

Combine sugar, milk, butter, salt and chocolate or cocoa in a saucepan. Cover and bring to a boil. Continue to boil until mixture reaches the soft ball stage, 234 to 238 degrees on a candy thermometer. Stir in vanilla and cool, without stirring, until fudge reaches room temperature. Beat until fudge becomes creamy, thick and holds its shape when dropped from a teaspoon. Drop by teaspoonfuls on wax paper or pour into a well-buttered 8"x8" baking dish. Cut into squares. Makes about one pound.

Snowflakes that stay on my nose and eyelashes, silver white winters that melt into springs...

-Oscar Hammerstein II

*Christmas holds many very special memories for me. As a little girl in the 1960's, I remember going to Grandma & Grandpa's store every Thursday evening with Mom, Dad and my brother to buy groceries. Grandpa was a butcher, but he liked to bake, too…chocolate pistachio cake was one of his favorite treats during the holidays. Each Christmas Eve we visited my grandparents' home. I can still remember the aluminum Christmas tree that sat in front of the dining room window. It had a rotating wheel and colors of red, blue, yellow and green would reflect on the glass ball ornaments hanging from the tree. Grandma & Grandpa celebrated their wedding anniversary on Christmas Eve and my parents were married on Christmas Eve, as well. To carry on this special tradition, my husband and I were married Christmas morning. I often wonder if our daughter will carry on this tradition which I hold dear.*

*Susan Copsey-Pearce*
*Gooseberry Patch*

# Memories

## Chocolate-Pistachio Cake

Combine cake and pudding mixes, orange juice, water, eggs and oil in a large mixing bowl; blend to moisten. Beat 2 minutes at medium speed, scraping bowl occasionally. Pour 3/4 of the batter into a greased and floured tube pan. Add syrup to remaining batter; mix well. Pour over batter in pan; don't stir. Bake at 350 degrees for one hour, then cool in pan on wire rack 10 minutes. Remove from pan and dust with powdered sugar. Makes 10 servings.

### Ingredients:

18-1/2 oz. pkg. white or yellow cake mix
3.4-oz. pkg. instant pistachio pudding mix
1/2 c. orange juice
1/2 c. water
4 eggs
1/2 c. oil
3/4 c. chocolate syrup
**Garnish:** powdered sugar

*Cinnamon candy wraps the air in spicy scents making it smell and feel like Christmas. Its bright red color with white powdered sugar reminds me of Christmas rubies under the snow and when I eat it, the warm tingling sensation is like tasting Christmas. I remember walking into our house and smelling the cinnamon candy my mom was making…I could almost taste it in the air. It reminded me of Christmas and the memories that come with it…a time away from the cares of the world spent with my family.*

*Jenny Sears*
*Denton, TX*

# Cinnamon Candy

1 c. powdered sugar      1 c. water
3-1/2 c. sugar           1 t. cinnamon oil
1 c. corn syrup          1 t. red food coloring

Line a 15"x13" baking sheet with foil; sprinkle evenly with powdered sugar. Place baking sheet on hot pads or trivets; set aside. In a heavy saucepan combine sugar, corn syrup and water. Cook over medium heat, stirring frequently, until mixture reaches 300 degrees on a candy thermometer. Remove from heat and stir in cinnamon oil and food coloring. Immediately pour on prepared baking sheet. When completely cool, break into pieces. Store in an airtight container. Makes about 2 pounds.

*Simple Christmas joys...caroling
door-to-door and being invited in for
Christmas cookies and steaming mugs
of cocoa; the smell of tangerines...Mom
always put one in the toes of our
stockings. I remember Grandma's jar
of ribbon candy and Great Grandma's
pans of cinnamon rolls wrapped in
newspaper to keep them warm.
Christmas as a child...trudging through
the snow up to Grandma & Grandpa's
house on Christmas Eve. Their tree
was in the front window strung with
bubble lights and draped in silver
icicles. Christmas cards bordered the
mirrors and archways. And best of
all, Grandma made her special
Russian teacakes.*

*Peggy Donnally
Toledo, OH*

# Memories

## Russian Teacakes

1 c. butter, softened
1/2 c. sugar
2 t. vanilla extract
2-1/4 c. all-purpose flour

1/4 t. salt
1 c. chopped pecans
1 to 2 c. powdered sugar

Cream butter, sugar and vanilla together; stir in flour, salt and pecans. Chill dough one hour. Roll teaspoonfuls of dough into onc-inch balls; bake at 350 degrees for 12 to 15 minutes on an ungreased baking sheet. Remove from oven and roll in powdered sugar; cool completely and roll in powdered sugar again. Makes 4 to 5 dozen.

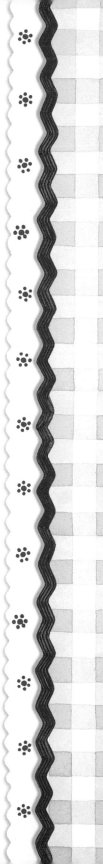

# Notes

# Gatherings

Magical moments with
family & friends...

*I simply love this time of year…falling snow
makes a swirling winter wonderland outside.
Inside, a crackling fire and the incredible
aromas coming from the kitchen warm our
hearts. Our entire family gathers…it's now
about 40 people! I love to make yummy treats
to share with our neighbors…it gives me such
a warm feeling inside. Even our sons' friends
drop by to ask if I've made any freshly baked
cookies that day. Each year, it's a tradition of
ours to make a special chocolate cake. My
two sons used to love to watch the mixer
incorporate all the ingredients as children,
but mostly they, along with my husband, look
forward to licking the batter bowl!*

*Erica Wieschenberg*
*Towaco, NJ*

# Gatherings

## Chocolate-Praline Cake

3  1-oz. sqs. bittersweet chocolate, finely chopped

1/3 c. baking cocoa

5 T. unsalted butter

1/3 c. oil

2/3 c. water

1 c. plus 2 T. sugar

1 egg, beaten

1-1/4 c. all-purpose flour

2 t. baking powder

1/3 c. buttermilk

Combine first five ingredients in a small saucepan; bring to a boil.
Stir constantly until smooth; remove from heat. Whisk sugar into
chocolate mixture until well blended. Transfer to a bowl; cool. Add egg;
set aside. Sift flour and baking powder together; add to chocolate
mixture, mixing well. Stir in buttermilk. Grease and flour a 9"
round cake pan lined with parchment paper. Butter paper and dust
with flour, removing any excess. Add batter; bake at 300 degrees for
45 to 50 minutes. Cool 5 minutes; invert on a rack to finish cooling.

## Topping:

8 oz. mascarpone cheese

3/4 c. plus 1-1/2 T. sugar,
   divided

1/4 c. water

1/2 c. almonds, chopped and
   toasted

1/2 c. hazelnuts, chopped and
   toasted

Blend together mascarpone and 1-1/2 tablespoons sugar; spread over
cooled cake. Combine remaining sugar and water together in a
saucepan; bring to a boil. Boil until mixture becomes golden; remove
from heat. Stir in nuts; pour on a foil-lined baking sheet. Cool, then
crush with a rolling pin. Sprinkle over cake. Makes 10 to 12 servings.

Here in Pennsylvania winters are long and family & friends mean everything. One of my fondest memories of Christmas is my Nanny's sand tart cookies. She would bake these favorites, but hide them until December 25th. Each year I would tip-toe up the stairway to the spare bedroom, the floor cold on my bare feet, and open the large wooden door to spy all the beautiful wrapped gifts on the big bed. On the dresser I could see a tin can…the lid was always hard to get off, but I knew inside would be neatly stacked cookies filled with the rich scent of cinnamon and brown sugar. My favorite Christmas memories…Nanny's cookies, getting scolded for eating too many before dinner and sitting on the sofa while grown-ups worked in the kitchen. A little girl, gazing sleepily at bubble lights on the tree, remembers the one little sand tart hidden in her pocket. Pulling out the pieces, I never dreamed they'd one day become such a fond memory.

Christi Miller
New Paris, PA

# Nanny's Sand Tart Cookies

4 c. brown sugar,
  packed
1 c. butter
4 eggs, divided
3 to 4 cups all-purpose
  flour

brown sugar and
  cinnamon to taste
3 c. walnut halves

Blend brown sugar, butter, 3 eggs and enough flour to make a soft dough. Wrap dough in wax paper and chill overnight. Roll dough on a lightly floured surface to 1/8-inch thickness and cut with cookie cutters. Beat remaining egg and brush over tops of cookies. Combine equal parts brown sugar and cinnamon and sprinkle over cookies; top each with a walnut half. Place on an ungreased baking sheet and bake at 350 degrees for 10 minutes. Makes 12 to 15 dozen.

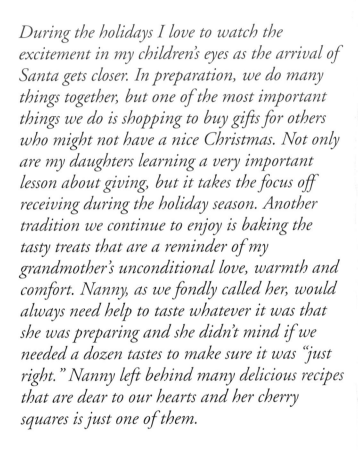

*During the holidays I love to watch the excitement in my children's eyes as the arrival of Santa gets closer. In preparation, we do many things together, but one of the most important things we do is shopping to buy gifts for others who might not have a nice Christmas. Not only are my daughters learning a very important lesson about giving, but it takes the focus off receiving during the holiday season. Another tradition we continue to enjoy is baking the tasty treats that are a reminder of my grandmother's unconditional love, warmth and comfort. Nanny, as we fondly called her, would always need help to taste whatever it was that she was preparing and she didn't mind if we needed a dozen tastes to make sure it was "just right." Nanny left behind many delicious recipes that are dear to our hearts and her cherry squares is just one of them.*

*Leigh Ann Doyle*
*Washington, PA*

# Gatherings

## Cherry Squares

Cream sugar and shortening together. Combine eggs and milk with a fork; reserve 3 tablespoons and set aside. Sift together flour, salt and baking soda; add egg and flour mixtures. Divide dough in half and place each half between 2 sheets of wax paper. Roll each into an 18"x12" rectangle. Remove wax paper and place on a greased 18"x12" baking sheet. Spoon pie filling over dough and top with remaining rectangle of dough, pressing edges to seal. Brush top with reserved milk mixture; sprinkle on nuts. Bake at 375 degrees for 35 to 40 minutes. Cut into squares. Makes 1-1/2 dozen.

### Ingredients:

- 1-1/2 c. sugar
- 1 c. shortening
- 3 eggs
- 3 T. milk
- 4 c. all-purpose flour
- 1 t. salt
- 1 t. baking soda
- 2  21-oz. cans cherry pie filling
- **Garnish: chopped nuts**

*Ever since our children were small we have enjoyed a homey tradition that they've not yet outgrown. Late Christmas Eve, all the children will put on their pajamas and snuggle in bed while my husband and I scurry around lighting candles, setting out platters of cookies and preparing root beer floats. When all the house is aglow, we each carry a candle upstairs, singing carols to each child…it's the signal that our celebration has begun. All seven children, as well as my husband and I, treasure this precious moment in time.*

*Shirley Agrimson*
*Peterson, MN*

Happiness starts at our own firesides.

-Douglas Terrold

# Gatherings

## Bon-Bon Cookies

1/2 c. butter
3/4 c. powdered sugar
1 T. vanilla extract
food coloring to desired
    color
1-1/2 c. all-purpose flour
1/8 t. salt

cream as needed
candied cherries, pitted
    dates, nuts, chocolate
    pieces to taste
Garnish: chopped nuts,
    flaked coconut, colored
    sugar

Mix first 3 ingredients and food coloring. Blend in flour and salt; mix with your hands. If dough is too dry, add a little cream. Measure out dough by tablespoonfuls and fill center with cherries, dates, nuts or chocolate. Bring dough up and around filling; pinch to seal. Bake one inch apart on an ungreased baking sheet at 350 degrees for 10 to 15 minutes; cool. Top with icing and garnish as desired.

## Icing:

1 c. powdered sugar
2 T. whipping cream

1 t. vanilla extract

Blend all ingredients together thoroughly.

*Being an oncology nurse is a very rewarding career; there is a special nurse-patient relationship that develops over the course of time. Many of my patients and their families have given me special ornaments and shared their favorite recipes during the holidays. Each Christmas I decorate a small tree adorned with all these ornaments and bake a fresh batch of cookies. It gives me the opportunity to reflect on each of their lives, not only the gift I hold in my hand, but the lessons they've taught me about life and living. This focus brings me simple joy at a very special time of year.*

*Jeanne Kenna*
*Ottsville, PA*

# Gatherings

## Theresa's Pressed Cookies

Cream together butter, cream cheese and sugar. Beat in egg yolk, vanilla and orange zest. Sift together dry ingredients and blend in butter mixture. Fill a cookie press with dough; press cookies on an ungreased baking sheet. Bake at 350 degrees for 12 to 15 minutes. Makes 6 to 7 dozen.

### Ingredients:

- 1 c. butter
- 3-oz. pkg. cream cheese
- 1 c. sugar
- 1 egg yolk
- 1 t. vanilla extract
- 1 t. orange zest
- 2-1/2 c. all-purpose flour
- 1/2 t. salt
- 1/4 t. cinnamon

Those who are Happiest are those who do the most for others.

— Booker T. Washington

181

*This past Christmas was extra-special because all my sons were home. I asked if they could get up early so we could have a nice breakfast together and open gifts before going to Grandma's house. There was some grumbling, but what a gift to me! We were all together promptly at 9:00 a.m., enjoyed a relaxing breakfast and took our time opening gifts. I will always remember that Christmas and the love and respect my sons showed to me by allowing us all to be together.*

*Kathy Grashoff*
*Ft. Wayne, IN*

I don't need to be rich,
my children
are my treasures.

-Myrna Jean Johnson

# Gatherings

## Apple Popover

**1/2 c. all-purpose flour**      **1/8 t. salt**
**1/2 c. milk**                   **4 egg whites**
**1 T. butter**

Spray an 8"x8" baking dish with non-stick vegetable spray; set aside. Beat flour and milk together with a wire whisk until thoroughly blended. Add butter, salt and egg whites; beat well again. Pour in baking dish and bake at 400 degrees for 25 to 30 minutes or until puffed and golden brown. Spoon on topping; cut in quarters. Makes 4 servings.

## Topping:

**1-1/2 c. apples, sliced**       **1/8 t. cinnamon**
**1/2 c. apple jelly**

Combine all ingredients in a saucepan over low heat. Stir until jelly is melted and mixture is heated throughout.

*The holidays are filled with celebrations, but we found little time to be together as a family. For this reason, we choose one evening as "Family Love Night" during the holiday season. We dress in our finest clothes, turn on the Christmas lights and light candles. Our children set the table and in the center are three small gifts. This evening there will be no interruptions. We treasure this time together as great memories are made. After dinner, we have one person at a time open one of the small gifts. Each has a piece of paper tucked inside with a question written on it. It might be, "Say something nice about the person to your right," or "What was one of your favorite memories of the past year?" After some lively conversation, our family sings songs and then we play a game or drive around to see the Christmas lights. It has come to be one of our most treasured nights of the year.*

*Barb Traxler*
*Mankato, MN*

# Angel Torte

6 egg whites
1/4 t. salt
1/2 t. cream of tartar
1-1/2 c. sugar
1/2 t. vanilla extract

Garnish: 12-oz. pkg.
whipped topping,
fresh berries or
raspberry pie filling

Beat together egg whites and salt until frothy; add cream of tartar and continue to beat at high speed until stiff. Gradually add sugar and vanilla. Spread mixture in a greased 13"x9" baking dish. Bake at 425 degrees for 3 minutes; turn off the oven, but do not open the door. Let the torte sit in the oven overnight or until oven cools completely. The torte will rise, then settle. Once torte has cooled, remove it from oven and cover with whipped topping and add fresh berries or pie filling on top. Refrigerate until serving. Makes 15 servings.

There are few holidays that Mom doesn't include someone who would otherwise be alone. She always takes on the responsibility to make sure everyone has a happy day filled with love. Of course, growing up, we didn't realize all she did until we were grown with families of our own. Today, with four enerations, she still manages to make each of us feel special and loved...our holidays are filled with joy and togetherness.

*Elena Tonkin*
*Powell, TN*

# Gatherings

## Fruit Cocktail Cake

2 c. sugar
2 c. all-purpose flour
2 eggs, beaten
2 t. baking soda

15-oz. can fruit cocktail, undrained
1/8 t. salt

Mix sugar, flour, eggs, baking soda, fruit cocktail and salt until well blended. Pour into a greased 13"x9" baking dish and bake at 350 degrees for 30 minutes. Cool, then top with warm icing.

### Icing:

1/2 c. margarine
1 c. evaporated milk
1 c. sugar

1/2 c. chopped nuts
1/2 c. flaked coconut
1 t. vanilla extract

Combine margarine, milk and sugar in a saucepan; boil 10 minutes. Remove from heat and add nuts, coconut and vanilla.

*Joy is being a mom of college children and cooking those special meals just for them when they're home for vacation. How wonderful it is to set the table and do a little extra to welcome them home. I still remember when my son came home from college, walked in the door and said, "Oh Mom, you've made my favorite pot roast...you know you're home when you smell that aroma coming from the kitchen." I think he melted my heart that day. A few years later I made the same meal when my daughter came home from her first semester. She walked in and said, "Oh thank you Mom for cooking one of my favorites." The funny thing is I didn't even tell her what I was cooking, but the memories came flooding back when the kitchen was filled with the aroma of a favorite childhood meal. I guess I've always had joy when I cook for my family.*

*Wendy Lee Paffenroth*
*Pine Island, NY*

# Gatherings

## Winter's Night Pot Roast

2 T. oil

2-1/2 to 3 lb. boneless
   chuck roast

1/4 t. salt

1 t. sugar

1/2 t. pepper

1/2 t. meat tenderizer

2 T. steak sauce

1/2 t. dried basil

1/2 t. dried thyme

4 c. water

5 potatoes, peeled and
   quartered

3 onions, peeled and
   quartered

4 carrots, peeled and sliced

flour

Pour oil in a Dutch oven over high heat. Add roast and brown
on all sides; sprinkle with salt, sugar, pepper and tenderizer.
Stir in steak sauce, basil, thyme and enough water to cover
roast. Bring to a boil, reduce heat and simmer, covered,
2 hours. Continue to add water to keep roast covered. Add
vegetables and continue to cook until tender. Remove one cup
liquid and add enough flour to create a thick mixture.
Remove meat and vegetables from Dutch oven, stir in flour
mixture and return meat and vegetables. Bring to a boil, then
remove from heat. Serves 6 to 8.

*For many years at Christmas, when I was a young teenager, we weren't able to be with our extended family. That very first year, my parents wanted to do something to fill the void of not having family close by. Their plan for that year has become a Christmas tradition for all of us. We always had Christmas dinner on Christmas Eve. This included many old family favorites and was served on Mom's best china. My parents always invited others who were alone at the holidays to this meal. This was one or two people, or sometimes a family. After dinner, we adjourned to the living room for a special evening. The program included each of the children presenting a poem, story or song. Our guests were always invited to take part, too. Sometimes they would tell us about Christmases of their past, favorite traditions or how they celebrated the holidays in their homeland. That evening always ended with the reading of the Christmas story from the Bible and a re-enactment by the children. As we grew, married and had children of our own, the grandchildren took part and we often had a baby in the family to play the part of Jesus. After the program, we would enjoy pie and Mom's special carrot pudding. After our guests departed, we would hang our stockings and go to bed. This simple tradition has grown to mean so much to all of us. We were never alone over the holidays and our family was able to give something to others.*

*Margaret Scoresby*
*Mount Vernon, OH*

# Gatherings

## Carrot Pudding

| | |
|---|---|
| 1/2 c. shortening | 1 t. salt |
| 1 c. brown sugar, packed | 1-1/4 t. cinnamon |
| 1 c. carrot, grated | 1/2 t. cloves |
| 1-1/2 c. apples, finely chopped | 1/2 t. nutmeg |
| 3/4 c. raisins | 1-1/2 t. baking powder |
| 1-1/2 c. all-purpose flour | |

Cream together shortening and sugar. Add carrots, apples and raisins; mix thoroughly. Sift together remaining ingredients and add to carrot mixture. Spoon into a buttered, 2-quart baking dish and bake, covered, at 325 degrees for 50 minutes. Serve warm with lemon sauce. Makes 8 to 10 servings.

## Lemon Sauce:

| | |
|---|---|
| 1 c. sugar | 1 egg, beaten |
| 1/2 c. butter | 3/4 t. lemon zest |
| 1/4 c. water | 4 T. lemon juice |

Combine all ingredients together in a saucepan. Heat to boiling; stirring occasionally.

*In Iowa, we always had a white Christmas and our family exchanged gifts on Christmas Eve after dinner. Chili was the perfect meal for a snowy Iowa night and Mom would start early in the day, letting it simmer for hours. Once the aroma was in the air, my sisters and I could hardly wait...it would soon be time to open presents! We would eat as quickly as possible and never asked for seconds, even if we were still hungry! Once we were done, we'd watch every bite Nana took. It seemed as if it took hours for her to finish. We hoped and prayed that she didn't want a second bowl, because we knew the rule...everyone had to be finished with dinner before we could begin. As soon as she took her last bite, we would grab her bowl before she could put her spoon down. I think Nana loved watching us wait for her to finish. We still have chili every Christmas Eve with each of our own families. Even if we can't all be together, the chili gives me the warm, cozy feeling of being home.*

*Susie Backus*
*Gooseberry Patch*

# Winter Wonderland Chili

1-1/2 lbs. ground beef, browned and drained

2  15-1/2 oz. cans light red kidney beans, undrained

15-1/2 oz. can dark red kidney beans, undrained

6-oz. can tomato paste

10-3/4 oz. can tomato soup

1 onion, diced

1 green pepper, diced

chili powder to taste

14-1/2 oz. can whole tomatoes, undrained

14-1/2 oz. can stewed tomatoes, undrained

Garnish: shredded Cheddar cheese and corn chips

Mix together ground beef, kidney beans, tomato paste, tomato soup, onion, green pepper and chili powder in a Dutch oven or stock pot. Use kitchen scissors to cut whole tomatoes while in the can; add with stewed tomatoes to ground beef mixture. Bring to a boil, reduce heat and simmer at least one hour. Garnish before servings. Makes 8 to 10 servings.

*Christmas in our family is the best time to bake all those wonderful recipes that have been passed down from generation to generation or even from friend to friend. Sometimes the aromas bring back the most wonderful memories and hopefully create more for those new little ones around us.*

*Rosalie Colby*
*Hiram, ME*

# Gatherings

## Mincemeat-Filled Cookies

Cream sugar and shortening; beat in eggs
and vanilla. Sift together flour, baking
powder and baking soda. Add dry mixture to
creamed mixture alternately with the milk;
chill dough one hour. Roll dough on a
floured surface to 1/8-inch thickness and cut
with a round cookie cutter. Place cookies on
a greased baking sheet and top each with a
teaspoonful of mincemeat; top with a second
cookie, crimping edges together. Bake at
450 degrees for 7 to 10 minutes or until
golden. Cool on a rack. Makes about
3 dozen.

### Ingredients:

**2 c. sugar**

**1 c. shortening**

**2 eggs**

**2 t. vanilla extract**

**5-1/2 c. all-
purpose flour**

**2 T. baking
powder**

**2 t. baking soda**

**1 c. milk**

**18-oz. jar prepared
mincemeat**

Growing up, each Christmas Eve we'd always drive around the neighborhood to see all of the holiday lights and decorations. It was a good way for my parents to "calm" my Christmas excitement. Now, we've followed the same tradition with our kids although times have changed…instead of hopping in a 1970's station wagon, we load everyone in the SUV!

*Gentry Barrett*
*Holly Springs, NC*

# Gatherings

## Yule Logs

2 8-oz. tubes refrigerated
   crescent rolls
8-oz. pkg. cream cheese,
   softened
1/4 lb. sausage, cooked
   and crumbled

1/8 t. salt
1 egg, beaten
1 to 2 T. poppy seed

Unroll each tube of crescent dough into a rectangle;
pressing to seal perforations. Combine cream cheese,
sausage and salt; spread mixture evenly over each rectangle
of dough. Starting with the long side, roll each rectangle
jelly roll-style, then pinch seams together. Slice each log
into one-inch pieces. Place slices on a greased baking sheet,
brush with egg and sprinkle with poppy seed. Bake at
375 degrees for 10 to 12 minutes. Makes 4 dozen.

*The Christmas of 2000, I started a new tradition. Our family arrived for a fun-filled day of eating, catching up and just being together again. We had all filled our plates with tasty goodies when Grandma squealed from the kitchen, "Santa's looking through the window!" Everyone stopped, listened and wondered, then there was a knock on the door. Santa himself came bounding in with a "Ho, Ho, Ho" and the children, as well as adults, just stared unbelieving. Santa soon found his way to the sofa, sat down and explained he had heard we were gathering gifts for another family, one whose Christmas might not be very bright. He said he would be honored if he could deliver our gifts, then as he opened a red velvet bag, each child carefully placed a gift inside. As they did this, Santa explained how very much their gift would mean to another child with no toys. Then, as Santa left, he asked us to sing a couple of his favorite songs. Somehow, I think Santa will make a stop at our home each and every year to help teach each one of us the happiness that comes from giving.*

*Michele Cutler*
*Sandy, UT*

# Gatherings

## Wassail

3 c. sugar
9 c. water, divided
5 cinnamon sticks

6 c. cranberry juice
3 c. orange juice
3 T. lemon juice

Combine sugar, 3 cups water and cinnamon sticks in a large stockpot; boil for 10 minutes. Add cranberry juice, remaining water, orange juice and lemon juice and heat through. Remove cinnamon sticks before serving. Makes about 20 servings.

Christmas joy to me is a simple celebration. Many years ago, when my children were very small, I began looking for a way to begin our own Christmas traditions. I wanted something we could do as a family that would be separate from the gifts and big meal at their grandparents' house Christmas day. So I planned a very simple meal for Christmas Eve…soup, rolls or muffins, ambrosia and cookies. After dinner, we read the Christmas story from the Bible and exchanged little gifts. Over the years, our celebration has changed but Christmas Eve dinner remains the same. Even though all our children are grown and married now, they still insist on the same simple meal.

Sara Tatham
Plymouth, NH

# Gatherings

## Christmas Eve Potato Soup

Combine potatoes and carrots in a stockpot, cover with water and bring to a boil. Cook until tender; drain. Sauté onion and celery in 2 tablespoons bacon drippings until tender, but not brown. Mix potatoes, carrots, onion, celery, salt, pepper and half-and-half in a stockpot and simmer for 30 minutes; do not boil. Spoon into serving dishes and garnish with crumbled bacon, parsley and cheese. Makes 4 to 6 servings.

Ah, how good
it feels!
The hand of an
old friend.

-Henry Wadsworth Longfellow

### Ingredients:

- 6 c. potatoes, sliced
- 1 c. carrots, sliced
- 6 slices bacon, crisply cooked and crumbled, drippings reserved
- 1 c. onion, chopped
- 1 c. celery, sliced
- salt and pepper to taste
- 2 c. half-and-half
- Garnish: fresh parsley sprigs and shredded Cheddar cheese

*I loved raising my family and have saved special items from my children's childhood. Now I am a grandmother of two little boys…what joy! Last year, one of my grandsons found a little Santa pin in the bottom of his stocking. His dad had worn it when he was only 2 years-old. The delight on his face as he pulled the string on the pin and Santa's nose lit up will remain with me always. I love surprising them with a special toy from the past. It makes me smile to know they think my attic is better than any store!*

*Janet Myers*
*Reading, PA*

# Golden Cheese Appetizers

8 T. butter

3-oz. pkg. cream
   cheese

4 oz. shredded sharp
   Cheddar cheese

3 egg whites, stiffly
   beaten

1/2 loaf French bread,
   cubed

Combine butter, cream cheese and Cheddar
cheese in a saucepan and heat until melted and
smooth. Fold in egg whites and blend well. Add
bread cubes to cheese mixture tossing well to coat.
Remove from saucepan and refrigerate, covered,
overnight. Place bread cubes on an aluminum
foil-lined baking sheet and bake at 350 degrees for
30 minutes or until golden brown. Makes 6 to
8 servings.

*What brings joy to my heart…Christmas music, a clear, star-sprinkled sky, a greeting card, just for fun shopping trips with a dear friend, cookie exchanges and surprises. The best simple joy; however, is time spent with my family. We cook, eat, laugh and just enjoy being together.*

*Joy McGruder*
*Chesterfield, MO*

# Gatherings

## Cherry Crumb Pie

30-oz. can cherry pie
    filling
1/2 t. almond extract

1/4 c. sugar
2 T. all-purpose flour
9-inch pie crust, unbaked

Combine pie filling and almond extract in a large bowl; set aside. Sift together sugar and flour and gently add to pie filling. Spoon into pie shell. Spread crumb topping over filling and bake at 400 degrees for 10 minutes. Reduce heat to 350 and bake for 30 minutes longer. Makes 6 to 8 servings.

## Topping:

1 c. all-purpose flour
1/2 c. brown sugar, packed
1/2 t. cinnamon

1/4 t. nutmeg
1/2 c. butter, melted and
    cooled

Mix together flour, brown sugar, cinnamon and nutmeg; stir in butter until well blended.

*No matter where we are on Christmas day, there's a tradition we've always held that brings our family joy…Christmas morning brunch. We always serve ham and scalloped potatoes for Christmas Eve dinner and, on Christmas morning, we have the leftovers, adding some eggs. Halfway through opening our presents, we stop to have our candlelight brunch. We all look forward to this time together as a family. It makes the morning last longer and gives us time to reflect on the true meaning of Christmas.*

*Jean Wieder*
*Orchard Park, NY*

# Gatherings

## Scalloped Potatoes

7 potatoes, peeled and
    thinly sliced
1/3 c. onion, finely
    chopped
1/3 c. all-purpose flour

1-1/2 t. salt
1/8 t. pepper
2-1/4 c. milk
3 T. butter
1/2 c. bread crumbs

Place half the potatoes in a greased 2-quart casserole dish;
top with half the onion. Sift together flour, salt and pepper;
add half to the casserole dish over the onion; repeat layers.
Pour milk over all, dot with butter and sprinkle on bread
crumbs. Bake, covered, at 350 degrees for 1-1/4 to
1-1/2 hours. Uncover and bake an additional 15 minutes.
Serves 6.

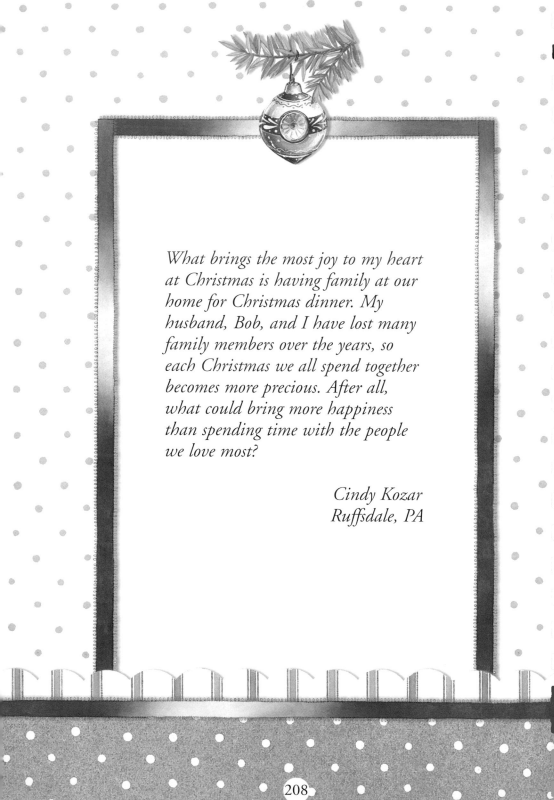

*What brings the most joy to my heart at Christmas is having family at our home for Christmas dinner. My husband, Bob, and I have lost many family members over the years, so each Christmas we all spend together becomes more precious. After all, what could bring more happiness than spending time with the people we love most?*

*Cindy Kozar*
*Ruffsdale, PA*

# Gatherings

# Mini Nut Cups

1-1/2 c. plus 3 T.
   margarine, softened

3 c. all-purpose flour

3  3-oz. pkgs. cream
   cheese

2-1/4 c. brown sugar,
   packed

3 eggs

3 c. chopped nuts

1/2 t. vanilla extract

Garnish: powdered
   sugar

Blend 1-1/2 cups margarine with flour and cream
cheese; shape into 72 small balls. Press each into
lightly greased mini muffin tins, shaping dough to
form a cup. Mix remaining margarine with brown
sugar, eggs, nuts and vanilla. Spoon one teaspoon into
each filled muffin tin. Bake at 375 degrees for 20 to
25 minutes or until edges are golden brown. Remove
from tins to cool and sprinkle with powdered sugar.
Makes 6 dozen.

Joy is that special sugar cookie recipe, long-yellowed by use and age. Joy is drinking cocoa from a Santa mug saved from childhood. Joy is searching for the perfect Christmas tree in the nearby forest and adorning it with sentimental ornaments. Joy is reading "T'was The Night Before Christmas" to kids of all ages. Joy is snow silently blanketing everything outside and the gathering of family & friends to share hugs and memories. To allow more time for the hugs and memories, our family has begun serving prime rib for Christmas dinner. While it slowly cooks and the aroma wafts throughout the house, we're able to relax and enjoy one another's company.

Debby Trapp
Baker City, OR

# Gatherings

## Juicy Prime Rib

1/4 c. black pepper
2 T. white pepper
2 T. salt
1-1/2 t. dried thyme

1-1/2 t. garlic powder
1 t. onion powder
8 to 10-lb. boneless beef
rib eye roast

Combine peppers, salt, thyme, garlic and onion powders; rub evenly over surface of roast. Place roast in a shallow roasting pan, insert a meat thermometer in the thickest part of the roast, being sure to avoid touching the bone. If preparing a medium-rare boneless rib eye roast, bake at 350 degrees for 13 to 15 minutes per pound, or until a meat thermometer reaches 150 degrees. For a medium roast, bake 16 to 18 minutes per pound, or 150 degrees on a meat thermometer. Tent roast with foil and let stand for 15 minutes before carving. Serves 16 to 20.

*Verenikas, cheese-filled dumplings, have always been a favorite recipe in our German family and my children would count on Grandma serving them when we visited during the Christmas holidays. My daughter spent time with Grandma during Christmas vacation just so she could learn how to make verenikas and carry on the family tradition. To my children, the mention of verenikas will always bring warm and loving memories of their grandmother.*

*Karen Olson*
*Vancouver, WA*

# Gatherings

## Old World Verenikas

Combine eggs, milk and one teaspoon salt. Gradually add 3 cups flour; stirring until a stiff dough forms. Knead until smooth. Roll dough very thin on a lightly floured surface; cut with a 2-1/2 inch round biscuit or cookie cutter. Stir together cottage cheese, remaining salt, cream, egg yolk and pepper in a mixing bowl. Place one tablespoon of cottage cheese mixture on half of each dough round. Fold over and pinch edges together. Fill a stockpot with water; bring to a boil. Boil verenikas for 8 to 10 minutes; drain. Transfer to a saucepan and fry in 3 tablespoons butter until golden brown on both sides. Melt remaining butter in a saucepan, add remaining flour and whisk. Pour evaporated milk into a 4-cup measuring cup, add enough water to equal 4 cups. Slowly add to flour mixture; bring to a boil. Serve over verenikas. Makes 3 to 4 servings.

### Ingredients:

- 3 eggs, beaten
- 1/2 c. milk
- 2 t. salt, divided
- 3 c. plus 3 T. all-purpose flour
- 1 pt. cottage cheese
- 2 T. cream
- 1 egg yolk
- 1/4 t. pepper
- 1/2 c. plus 3 T. butter
- 12-oz. can evaporated milk

*During the first week in December I send invitations for friends to join me for a Christmas tea. I ask each of them to bring a Christmas story, poem or personal remembrance to share. After we spend time enjoying one another's company, then we go to the dining room where everyone can make an ornament to take home; afterward we have dessert and coffee. We all love spending time together and for me, this is one way I can show my friends how much I appreciate them.*

*Pat Crandall*
*Rochester, NY*

# Gatherings

## Sour Cream Pound Cake

1 c. butter, softened
3 c. sugar
6 eggs
1 c. sour cream

1/4 t. baking soda
3 c. all-purpose flour
1 t. vanilla

Mix ingredients together with an electric mixer; pour batter into a well-greased and floured tube pan. Bake at 325 degrees for 1-1/2 hours or until a toothpick inserted in the middle comes out clean. Let cool 10 minutes in pan; remove. Makes 10 servings.

*One of the most difficult things to do during the Christmas season is to step back and recapture the simple joys of the holiday. In our family, we've chosen to find alternatives to commercial gift giving and opt instead for home baked or handmade gifts. Not only do these gifts provide our family with the opportunity to share the holiday spirit, but it shows us that we all care enough to take the time to make something special.*

*Elizabeth McKay*
*Romeoville, IL*

# Almond Roca

**1-1/2 c. almonds, finely chopped**

**16-oz. bittersweet or semi-sweet chocolate, finely chopped**

**1 lb. butter**

**2 c. sugar**

Spread almonds evenly on a lightly greased baking sheet and toast in a 350 degree oven for 10 minutes; stirring halfway through. Remove half the almonds from the baking sheet; set aside. Spread remaining almonds evenly over the baking sheet and top with half the chocolate; set aside. Combine butter and sugar in a heavy saucepan. Heat over medium heat, stirring constantly, until candy thermometer reads 310 degrees. Quickly pour mixture evenly over nuts and chocolate on baking sheet. Top with remaining nuts and chocolate. Chill, uncovered, for one hour. When cool, break into pieces and store between sheets of wax paper in an airtight container. Makes approximately 1-1/2 pounds.

*I have many wonderful and fond memories of being with my family at Christmas. As a child, at home with my parents, brother and sisters, we would be wide awake at 5 a.m. ready to run down the stairs to see what Santa had brought us! Mom & Dad would then get us all dressed in our finest and we'd be off to Christmas mass. After mass, we went straight to Grammy's house where we'd open gifts and have a traditional turkey dinner with all the trimmings. The aroma of pine, roasting turkey and bread baking were heavenly to me, but what I loved most of all were the dozens of Christmas cookies perfectly arranged on trays…just waiting for 5 little pairs of hands to pick up all they could carry! Not only were they delicious, but beautifully baked and decorated. To this day the most joyful thing about Christmas is being with my family and continuing the Christmas cookie tradition.*

*Brenda Dickson*
*Overland Park, KS*

218

# Gatherings

## Buttery Almond Cookies

1 c. butter
1/3 c. sugar
1 t. vanilla extract
1 t. almond extract
2 t. cold water
2 c. all-purpose flour

1 c. almonds, finely chopped
Garnish: colored sugar, nonpareils, sprinkles, and sugar

Cream butter and sugar together; stir in vanilla and almond extracts. Blend in water, then stir in flour until just mixed. Add almonds and chill dough 2 hours or overnight. Form dough into one-inch balls; then roll in colored sugar, sprinkles or nonpareils. Place on an ungreased baking sheet and flatten balls with the bottom of a glass that's been dipped in sugar. Bake at 325 degrees for 20 minutes or until just firm to the touch; don't overbake. Cool on baking sheet one minute, then remove to a wire rack to cool completely. Makes about 3 dozen.

# Index

# Index

Notes

# Send us your favorite memory

## ...and a recipe that has special meaning to you!

Just like the original **Gooseberry Patch** cookbooks that you've come to know and love, our new Simple Joys books will be filled with inspirational remembrances, tried & true recipes, magical watercolors and...joy! If we select your memory & recipe for a Simple Joys cookbook, your name will appear right along with it and...you'll receive a **FREE** copy of the book! Mail to:

**Gooseberry Patch**
600 London Road
Department Book
Delaware, Ohio 43015

Recall it as often as you wish, a Happy Memory never wears out.
-Victor Borge

**Phone us:**
1·800·854·6673

**Fax us:**
1·740·363·7225

**Visit our website:**
www.gooseberrypatch.com

We'll send you our latest catalog with lots of goodies including our best-selling cookbooks!

Notes